THE POET'S GIFT

THE POET'S GIFT

Toward the Renewal
of Pastoral Care

DONALD CAPPS

Westminster/John Knox Press
Louisville, Kentucky

Book design by Laura Lee

First edition

Published by Westminster/John Knox Press
Louisville, Kentucky

This book is printed on acid-free paper that meets the American National Standards Institute Z39.48 standard. ∞

PRINTED IN THE UNITED STATES OF AMERICA
9 8 7 6 5 4 3 2 1

Library of Congress Cataloging-in-Publication Data

Capps, Donald.
   The poet's gift : toward the renewal of pastoral care / Donald Capps. — 1st ed.
     p.   cm.
   Includes bibliographical references and index.
   ISBN 0-664-25403-9 (alk. paper)

   1. Pastoral counseling.   2. Religion and poetry.   3. Levertov, Denise, 1923–   .   4. Stafford, William, 1914–   .   5. Pastoral theology.   I. Title.
BV4012.2.C2746   1993
253—dc20

                                       93-9307

to Karen
who worries for us

CONTENTS

ACKNOWLEDGMENTS

I want to thank James Lapsley and Christie Neuger, my former colleagues in Pastoral Theology at Princeton Theological Seminary, for making it possible for me to have a semester's leave in the fall of 1991 to write this book. I also want to thank Lydia Anderson and Paul Reigstad for encouraging my interest in poetry during my high school and college days. I am especially grateful to James E. Dittes for being a supportive mentor and friend, and to Anne Hiebert Smith, whose public demonstrations of movement therapy inspired the argument I develop in chapter 2. Jeffries Hamilton, my editor at Westminster/John Knox Press, was enormously helpful in shepherding this manuscript through the review process. Danielle Alexander coordinated production, Jo-Ann Young and Katy J. Monk edited the manuscript, and John Capps prepared the index. The inspiration for this book was Joseph Sittler, a senior member of the Divinity School faculty at the University of Chicago when I was its most junior member. Joe was not only my sponsor for ordination in the Lutheran Church in America but also living testimony to the fact that the Christian apologist can be a lover and user of poetry. This book is a small token of gratitude to my wife, Karen, for her friendship throughout the years. I cannot imagine life without her.

Grateful acknowledgment is made for permission to reprint the following copyrighted material:

The poems "Mother's Day," "A Memorial for My Mother," "1932," "A Life, a Ritual," "Learning How to Lose," "Scripture," "Serving with Gideon," "Madge," "Stillborn," "Waiting in Line," "Not Having Wings," "The Book About You," "Scars," "Barnum and Bailey," "What If We Were Alone?" "By Tens," "Ultimate Problems," and "The Dean at Faculty Retreat" are from *An Oregon Message* by William Stafford. Copyright © 1987 by William Stafford. Reprinted by permission of HarperCollins Publishers.

The poems "Passwords," "For a Lost Child," "Disposal," "Rescue," "Consolations," "It's All Right," "The Gospel Is Whatever Happens," "Waiting for God," "Local Events," "You Don't Know the End," and "In Camp" are from *Passwords* by William Stafford. Copyright © 1991 by William Stafford. Reprinted by permission of Harper-Collins Publishers.

The poems "Parentage," "In Fear and Valor," "Vacation Trip," "Some Shadows," "Listening," "Vocation," "At the Grave of My Brother," "Aunt Mabel," "A Family Turn," "Thinking for Berky," "At Liberty School," "The Girl Engaged to the Boy

Who Died," "Judgments," "Back Home," "Existences," "The Wanderer Awaiting Preferment," "Fifteen," "Bess," "Circle of Breath," "Elegy," "Father's Voice," "A Gesture Toward an Unfound Renaissance," "For a Child Gone to Live in a Commune," "The Only Card I Got on My Birthday Was from an Insurance Man," "Strokes," "Adults Only," "Bi-Focal," "At the Bomb Testing Site," "At the Salt Marsh," "Traveling Through the Dark," "Chickens the Weasel Killed," "Behind the Falls," "Watching the Jet Planes Dive," "Like a Little Stone," "Earth Dweller," "Vespers," "Walking West," "The Tillamook Burn," "Sunset: Southwest," "Freedom," "The Little Ways That Encourage Good Fortune," "Outside," "Allegiances," "Monuments for a Friendly Girl at a Tenth Grade Party," "Connections," "A Ritual to Read to Each Other," "A Walk in the Country," "A Message from the Wanderer," and "Religion Back Home" are from *Stories That Could Be True* by William Stafford. Copyright © 1977 by William Stafford. Reprinted by permission of the author.

The poems "Ruby Was Her Name," "My Mother Was a Soldier," "Our Kind," "Remembering Brother Bob," "A Catechism," "One Time," "Dark Wind," "In a Corner," "Murder Bridge," "Revelation," "Yellow Flowers," "Confessor," "A Day to Remember," "Not Very Loud," and "There Is Blindness" are from *A Glass Face in the Rain* by William Stafford. Copyright © 1982 by William Stafford. Reprinted by permission of the author.

The poems "Too Easy: to write of Miracles" and "Who He Was" are reprinted from Denise Levertov: *Collected Earlier Poems 1940–1960*. Copyright © 1957, 1958, 1959, 1960, 1961, 1979 by Denise Levertov.

The poems "A Common Ground," "A Solitude," "A Cure of Souls," "The Old Adam," "Abel's Bride," "A Man," and "The Mutes" are reprinted from Denise Levertov: *Poems 1960–1967*. Copyright © 1958, 1959, 1960, 1961, 1963, 1964, 1965, 1966 by Denise Levertov.

The poems "Despair," "The Heart," "July 1968," "He-Who-Came-Forth," "Prologue: An Interim," "A Defeat in the Green Mountains," "Joie de Vivre," "The Malice of Innocence," "A New Year's Garland," and "Olga Poems" are reprinted from Denise Levertov: *Poems 1968–1972*. Copyright © 1965, 1966, 1967, 1968, 1969, 1970, 1971 by Denise Levertov Goodman.

The poems "A Woman Alone," "A Daughter," "Death Psalm," "The Blue Rim of Memory," "The Emissary," "Movement," "A Wanderer," and "A Soul-Cake" are reprinted from Denise Levertov: *Life in the Forest*. Copyright © 1975, 1976, 1977, 1978 by Denise Levertov.

The poems "The Mourner," "Of Necessity," "Vocation," and ". . . That Passeth All Understanding" are reprinted from Denise Levertov: *Oblique Prayers*. Copyright 1981, 1982, 1983, 1984 by Denise Levertov.

The poems "Poet and Person," "The Passing Bell," "Visitant," "The Acolyte," and "Beginners" are reprinted from Denise Levertov: *Candles in Babylon*. Copyright © 1978, 1979, 1980, 1981, 1982 by Denise Levertov.

Acknowledgments

The poems "To R.D.," "Annunciation," "Wings in the Pedlar's Pack," and "Inheritance" are reprinted from Denise Levertov: *A Door in the Hive*. Copyright © 1984, 1987, 1988, 1989 by Denise Levertov.

The poems "To Olga," "During a Son's Dangerous Illness," "Urgent Whisper," "She wept, and the women consoled her," and "I learned that her name was Proverb" are reprinted from Denise Levertov: *Breathing the Water*. Copyright © 1984, 1985, 1986, 1987 by Denise Levertov.

The poems "Stele," "Broken Pact," "Time for Rivets," "The Opportunity," "The Batterers," "Hoping," "Misnomer," "Witnessing From Afar," and "Suspended" are from Denise Levertov: *Evening Train*. Copyright © 1990, 1991, 1992 by Denise Levertov.

INTRODUCTION

I N RECENT YEARS, MUCH HAS BEEN WRITTEN TO SUPPORT A NARRATIVE APPROACH
to pastoral care. Building on the observation that pastoral care typically
involves the hearing and telling of personal stories, a number of authors
have made the point that pastoral care involves helping individuals, couples,
and families to locate their personal stories within the framework of the
Christian story.[1]

In my own work, I have been attracted to a particular type of story—the
parable—because this was the story form that Jesus used to communicate his
own understanding of how God is acting, and *not* acting, in human lives.
Given the subversive nature of the parable,[2] our use of it to inform our
interpretations of our own life experience leads to some surprising conclusions
about how our personal stories relate to the Christian story. When a parable is
used to interpret our own lives, the dilemmas or difficulties we face ourselves,
it usually opens up a surprising solution, an unexpected and unanticipated
approach to the resolution of our dilemmas and difficulties.

It has also become increasingly clear to me that the acts of pastoral care
performed by pastors in the parish context are very similar to Jesus' parables:
these acts usually involve brief, time-compressed encounters and often occur
in the context of a life crisis having to do with a family or vocational
problem.

Of course, many such pastoral encounters occur against the backdrop of an
ongoing relationship between pastor and parishioner. In many cases, this
relationship spans a period of many years. In this sense, any single pastoral
encounter is one episode in a story having novelistic characteristics. Yet the
geographical mobility of parishioners and pastors, the denominational mobility of parishioners who move from one church to another, and the changes in
family configuration that we have witnessed in recent years have significantly
altered the conditions that have traditionally supported such novelistic
narrative experience. In general, pastors no longer have the long-term,

1

in-depth relationships with a family that were the norm in the nineteenth and early twentieth centuries, when the modern novel itself came into its own.

For better or worse, our situation today is more akin to that of Jesus in first-century Palestine, where the mutual expectations that had bound individuals to family and place of birth could no longer be assumed. Reflective of this very change are Jesus' own attitudes toward family relationships: "Who are my mother and my brothers? Whoever does the will of God is my brother, and sister, and mother." In such a social setting, life itself is more parabolic than novelistic. Significant personal encounters continue to occur, but they are less routine, more haphazard, accidental, and episodic, much like the episodes that Jesus relates in his parables and that the Gospels relate about Jesus' own ministry as he went from place to place.

My purpose in this book, however, is not to repeat myself with further advocacy of the parabolic approach to pastoral care. I have already devoted major portions of three books to this subject.[3] What I propose to do here instead is to focus on the work of contemporary parabolists—poets—and explore the relevance and significance of their work for pastoral care.

Among contemporary literary genres, the modern poem is the most direct descendant of the parable. Like the parable, the poem is typically much briefer and more compressed than the novel or short story. Like the parable and unlike the novel, the poem is episodic, usually concerned with a single life event or experience, with little or no attempt to explain how this event or experience fits within the larger life structure of the poet or the poet's subject. Unlike the novel and the short story, the poem does not take the trouble to develop in detail the life story of its major character. Instead, the person in the poem—usually the poem's "I" or implied "Self"—is revealed within the framework of the poem itself, in relation to the event or scene that is the subject of this particular poem.

Like the parable, the poem is an extended metaphor, the meaning of which is expressed by the poem itself. Like the parable, one does not look outside the poem for the "point" of the poem, since the poem is the point. Too, like the parable, the poem is necessarily open-ended. Its goal is not to tell a complete story, as a novel does, but to use a life episode—often one that is seemingly unimportant or that other, less perceptive eyes would have overlooked—to inspire or even prod the reader to look at life in a different way. Like Jesus' parables, poems are usually considered unorthodox, if not radical, precisely because they challenge our usual and routine ways of perceiving and construing our life experiences, enticing us into viewing them from a different angle or slant.

More could be said about the similarities between ancient parables and contemporary poems, but I have said enough to indicate how this book extends my previous efforts to explore the relationships between pastoral actions and texts,[4] especially texts that tell a story. This book is also an extension of my earlier position that an ongoing relationship between the pastor and parishioner (one analogous to the therapist-client relationship) is not necessarily the key to the effectiveness of the pastoral action, as is usually argued by those who advocate a narrative approach to pastoral care and counseling.[5] Instead, I would argue that there is power in the episodic, in chance encounters between relative strangers; I submit that the effectiveness of such encounters has less to do with personal relationships as such and more to do with whether the encounter leads the participants to break their usual ways of framing events, locating them instead within a radically different frame of meaning.

The Poet's Gift is an invitation to consider poetry as a source of vision and inspiration for the pastoral task and as a source of renewal, not only for the ministry of individual pastors but also for the field of pastoral care itself. This book recognizes that there is a certain affinity between poets and pastors. The tendency of poets to be explorative, questioning, and tentative, though not spineless or without conviction and a passion for truth, has a natural fit with the kinds of human experiences that have been of greatest concern to pastoral care, and with the ways that pastors, in confronting these situations, have found themselves responding to them. Again and again, pastors confess that they have been unable to communicate a theological "answer" to a parishioner in distress, not because the pastor did not know what such an answer would be but because this answer would violate the experience itself, usually by imposing greater certainty or clarity onto the experience than the parishioner and the pastor felt was warranted at the time. In such situations, pastors have much in common with poets. In turn, poets who write about the anomalies, the tragedies, and the unexpected blessings of life have much in common with pastors, as they devote considerable attention to such experiences and write about them in much the same way that pastors speak of them: with the head but also with the heart, with thoughtfulness but also with passion, with mental intensity but also with deep emotion.

Poets and pastors also share a preference for language that is "experience-near," that speaks of human experience in the concrete, and not from some ivory tower or privileged distance. Given their investment in lived human experience, both poets and pastors exhibit unusual care for how words are used and what words communicate. Poets struggle—often for days and weeks—to find just the right word, the right phrase. In much the same way, pastors who take their pastoral care work seriously are deeply concerned with how things are said, and with why *this* rather than *that* word or phrase was chosen in a given context. An important clue to whether a seminarian or beginning pastor is likely to become a really effective pastoral care person is that he or she exhibits a deep care for words, using them carefully, even lovingly, and attending to why certain words communicate well while others do not. Our use of the "verbatim" (the case study report) in seminary courses and Clinical Pastoral Education is testimony to our conviction that words *do* matter, that poorly chosen words have the power to hurt and that well-chosen words have the power to heal. Like poets, good pastoral care persons do not treat words like idols—they are not to be venerated but to be used—yet they do struggle to find the right things to say, and to discover the most appropriate word or phrase among the many words or phrases that others, less scrupulous in their choice and use of language, would have judged to be "good enough."

Occasionally, especially when the nation is at war or undergoing some major catastrophe, our poets will speak as a community of voices, each adding his or her voice to a chorus of common concern for human suffering and a common longing for peace on earth. Each speaks in a highly individualistic way, yet contributes his or her unique gift to a larger purpose. In this view of the poet—as one voice among others—my original plan was to use the work of quite a number of poets. In this way, the book would reflect the considerable regional, cultural, and gender diversity that is found among American poets. As the book began to take shape in my mind, however, I realized that it would be impossible to do justice to the richness of individual poets if only one or two of their poems were included in this book.

So I have chosen to focus on the poetry of only two contemporary American poets: Denise Levertov and William Stafford. Their work has led me to conclude that poetry speaks to the same life issues that pastors are concerned with and that poetry's manner of addressing these issues can be instructive for pastors. With these two poets, something of the regional, cultural, and gender diversity of the community of American poets will at least be exhibited, as Levertov and Stafford have lived in different regions of the country, and spent their early years in very different cultural contexts (Levertov in a suburb of London and Stafford in small towns in Kansas). And, of course, they have experienced and written about life from the perspectives their genders have afforded them. Religion, too, has had a significant place in their poetry, as both have been sustained throughout their lives by their respective religious legacies (Levertov is the daughter of an Anglican priest, her father, a Russian Jew, having converted to Christianity as a young man, and Stafford was brought up in a traditional Midwestern Protestant home, though it was not until he was in college that he began his lifelong commitment to Christian pacifism).

Although Levertov and Stafford have very different backgrounds, their poems share the qualities of being both personal and direct. I am struck time and again by the fact that both avoid flowery language and frequent literary allusions and instead write in direct, unpretentious language about common human experiences. Through such directness, they enable the reader to see and to feel the deeper levels of such experience, and thus to gain a more vital appreciation for the fact that, in our everyday human existence, there is always far more there than meets the eye. These deeper levels are, of course, what pastors are mindful of in their caring for others. While it is intrinsic to poetry that it seeks to disclose and explore these deeper levels of human experience, and Levertov and Stafford are surely not unique in this regard, a chronological reading of their work reveals that they have struggled throughout their careers to find more and more effective ways of disclosing the deeper levels of human experience, including their own, and that dissatisfaction with their previous efforts continues to fuel their work and give it the uniquely restless, exploratory quality that it has. In this regard, their poetry exemplifies the satisfactions and the frustrations that pastors also attest to as they, too, struggle to find more effective ways to open themselves and others to the deeper levels of human experience, so that they and their parishioners may live—if only for a few moments—in the place where hearts are opened and souls become transparent to self and others.

When I read Levertov and Stafford, I sense the same passion to probe and understand what is occurring beneath the surface—qualities that pastors also exhibit, especially when pastors speak in frustration and anger about the superficiality of much of what takes place in their daily ministry, even on those occasions when they are engaged in acts of pastoral care. By focusing on these poets, we will see that such frustration and anger are not at all unique to pastors; this is something that poets also experience and write about with considerable frequency. We will also see how they have addressed this problem and found ways—through language—to overcome it. Both their frustrations and their successes can be instructive for pastors who are beset with the same frustrations and are in search of ways, largely through the medium of language, to create openings so that there may be greater opportunity for genuine self-disclosure as parishioners and pastors tell their stories, one to another.

The poetry of Levertov and Stafford is being used here to make a point, which is that poetry is a valuable resource for pastoral care precisely because poets and pastors have so much in common. This means that I do not approach their poetry as a literary critic might, exploring why such-and-such poem works well and such-and-such poem does not; nor do I approach their work as one primarily interested in the nature and function of poetic discourse. These are not my concerns. What interests me are the obvious affinities between poetry and pastoral care—affinities that have occasionally been noted, as when pastors have given a parishioner a book of poems to read, but have never been systematically explored, as I attempt to do here. Thus, the reader should not expect to be treated here to the penetrating analyses of poems and poetic discourse that the literary critic offers. On the other hand, I hope to take us beyond the current state of the art—in which poetry is viewed mainly as a potentially valuable resource for a parishioner who is sick or troubled to read—and to show that poetry can inform our understanding of what pastoral care is all about. If, in the end, I fail to persuade my readers that I am onto something here, I will at least have done something of considerable value for myself, as I will have written about two human capacities that fill me with almost unspeakable awe: the gift of inspired poetry and the gift of inspired pastoral caring.

The first three chapters of this book, two centering on Stafford's poetry and one on Levertov's, deal with some long-standing issues in pastoral care, including the significance of personal self-awareness for engaging in pastoral care; the role of attentive listening as an essential feature of all pastoral care encounters; and the pastor's role in assisting others in grieving over losses. The remaining two chapters are a response, in a sense, to calls now being made, as Charles V. Gerkin puts it, for us to "widen the horizons" of pastoral care,[6] especially to take into account a wider range of human experience, and to expand our theological models to accommodate this expanded vision. The first of these two remaining chapters, focused on the poetry of Levertov, addresses the family crucible in which her personal and poetic self was formed, and our need, as pastoral care persons, to hear women's accounts of their lives with the respect and sensitivity they deserve. The final chapter, based on Stafford's work, makes the case for a further expansion of our pastoral care perspective to include the whole created order. These two chapters reflect my own efforts to listen to and for the winds of change currently blowing in the field of pastoral care. They are an implicit endorsement of the work of the newer—as well, of course, of some of the older—generation of pastoral theologians.

1. The Self We Bring to Our Vocation

GARY HARBAUGH'S BOOK, *THE PASTOR AS PERSON*, BEGINS WITH THESE words: "Pastors are persons. Most of the problems pastors experience in the parish are not caused by the pastor forgetting he or she is a pastor. Most difficulties pastors face in the parish arise when the pastor forgets that he or she is a person."[1] In successive chapters, Harbaugh explores the various dimensions of the "whole" person, including the physical, the thinking, the feeling, the relating, and the choosing person, and shows how they are interrelated and how they interact in the daily conduct of ministry. Throughout, he emphasizes that each pastor is a person in his or her own right and that denial of this simple but important fact can lead to serious problems in one's ministry.

I want to build on Harbaugh's insights in this chapter by focusing on one important implication of the fact that each pastor is a unique person, namely, that one's pastoral care ministry is profoundly informed by one's awareness of who he or she is. In what he terms his most personal chapter in the book, "The Pastor as a Choosing Person," Harbaugh tells us that he came to the realization that he needed to make choices in his life and his ministry, and that making choices always entails risk. This new self-understanding had a profound impact on his own ministry, for previously he had operated on the assumption that he did not need to make choices, that he could do everything. By viewing himself as a person who had to make some choices, and recognizing that choosing entails risk, he also discovered what it means to live one's life according to grace, for in becoming a choosing person, he could no longer claim to be omnicompetent.

Harbaugh's personal discovery that it was vital for him to become a choosing person was an important achievement in self-awareness. As he freely confesses, it did not solve all of his problems, for he continues to this day in his struggle with needing to be a choosing person. Yet this insight he gained into himself was invaluable. It has influenced his ministry ever since. Indeed, he points out that, rather than making him a more cautious and controlled minister, it has had the opposite effect, as he is now more willing and able to take risks and to exercise greater freedom.

Like Harbaugh in his chapter on the choosing person, poets often write autobiographically, relating personal experiences through their poems. Also like Harbaugh, as they reflect on their lives, poets often discover deep insights into their inner selves, and such insights are frequently revealed through their poetry. Such achievements in self-knowledge, in turn, become important for their subsequent work, as poems written later bear the mark of these earlier achievements in self-knowing. In effect, poets' own work reveals the importance for their work of new discoveries in self-knowledge. If such discoveries did not occur from time to time, their poetry would lose its creative edge. It would become repetitive, a mere imitation of earlier work.

Denise Levertov's work provides an excellent illustration of this process. In commenting on the fact that her poetry took a decidedly political turn in the 1960s, she says she found it necessary "to explain to myself what I was doing." On the one hand, she "spent a lot of time attempting to define what qualities can make 'political' poetry work as poetry, to defend such poetry from attacks made from a position of rigid, general aesthetic objection rather than on a case by case basis." On the other hand, her very immersion in the "ocean of crisis in which we swim" strengthened her affinity for poetry which is "in search of significance underneath and beyond the succession of temporal events: a poetry which attests to the deep spiritual longing that . . . is increasingly manifest in recent American verse."[2]

It is more difficult to identify a critical turn in William Stafford's work. The form of his poetry has not changed very much through the years, and the content of his later poems is quite similar to his earlier work. Yet both poets assume a kind of personal identity in the course of their work, identities similar to Harbaugh's understanding of himself as a "choosing person." In Stafford's case, the term that he frequently uses to describe himself is "the wanderer." For Levertov, there is a recurring affirmation of herself as one who gains strength through solitude. These self-designations arise out of their personal struggles to know themselves. While these self-identifications do not capture the whole person, they do express what the poet considers to be a central aspect of who he or she is, especially within the framework of the poetry itself. Thus, even as Harbaugh relates his self-designation as "choosing person" primarily to his work and role as a pastor, so Stafford and Levertov's self-designations have particular relevance to their work as poets. When he is about his work as a poet, Stafford expresses himself as a "wanderer." When Levertov is about her work as a poet, she senses that, in this aspect of her life, she is a woman who derives sustenance—personal and spiritual—from "O blessed Solitude."

Harbaugh notes that his use of the Myers-Briggs Type Indicator* has helped him with many of the dimensions of a holistic approach to himself and his ministry, "but something beyond the Myers-Briggs is needed to help with our integration of our past into our present situation. Seminarians often bring to their studies some heavy burden from early life experiences with the family and sometimes with the church. . . . Since so little time is spent in seminary with the healing of hurtful memories of the past, it is probable that most of the seminarian's 'unfinished business' is taken into the parish."[3] He suggests that journaling can help people identify and work through "unfinished business" from the past so that they may be more fully and freely available for ministry in the present.

Reading poetry is also a helpful way for us to identify and work through the unfinished business of the past, as a poem often reveals the poet's struggle to identify and work through his or her own unfinished business. Poets write about their childhoods, their parents and grandparents, their brothers and sisters, and their childhood friends and schoolmates, and they are often willing to disclose what their family life was like, even to the extent of revealing some very painful family secrets. They do this because they understand that these early experiences and the unfinished business reflected therein not only are of crucial importance to their adult lives in general, but also have bearing, specifically, on their vocation as poets. Thus, by reading poetry, we can observe how other individuals have struggled with the unfinished business of their childhood and youth, and how these early life experiences continue to have impact on their vocation today.

By focusing on their own early experiences, poets also teach us that family and neighborhood have a formative influence on our lives, even as adults, especially in the choices and commitments we make in personal relationships and vocation. Yet poets also insist on their own unique individuality and on the role that their personal tendencies and gifts have played from a very early age in the formation of their lives. They affirm the importance of the "environment," but they also insist on the influence of personal, dispositional factors which are not attributable to environmental influence alone.

---

*Myers-Briggs Type Indicator® is a registered trademark of Consulting Psychologists Press, Inc.

In this chapter, we will focus on William Stafford's formative years and will see both how he has used his vocation as a poet to assist him in his exploration into his past, and how his past provides resource material for his work as a poet now. By attending to the poems that focus on his early years, we will gain valuable insight into how the "unfinished business" of his early years has continued to play a role in his work throughout his adult life, both as stimulus and impediment. We will also see why it was necessary, if not inevitable, that he become "the wanderer."

My hope, of course, is that by focusing on Stafford's explorations into his own early years, readers, especially seminarians, will be prompted to engage in similar exercises in self-reflection, with particular attention given to how the unfinished business of their formative years continues to play a role in their own vocational choices and commitments. Some readers may discover, in the course of these self-reflections, that they are able to find a self-designation similar to those of Stafford and Levertov, one that enables them to recognize what makes them unique among others who have chosen—or been chosen for—the same calling. If it reflects genuine self-knowledge, such a self-designation can be an important resource for us as we consider how we will make our own selfhood felt in the enactment of our vocation.

THE MAKING OF A WANDERER

William Stafford was born in Hutchinson, Kansas, in 1914, and studied at the University of Kansas and the University of Iowa, where he received his doctorate. A conscientious objector during World War II, he worked in Forest Service and Soil Conservation camps, and after the war, he served with the Brethren Service Commission and Church World Service. He joined the faculty of Lewis and Clark College in Portland, Oregon, in 1948, and was Professor of English there until his retirement in 1980. He and his wife, Dorothy, whom he married in 1944, are the parents of four children.

His first major collection of poems, *West of Your City*, was published in 1960. *Traveling Through Dark* won the 1962 National Book Award for poetry. *The Rescued Year* appeared in 1966, *Allegiances* in 1970, *Someday, Maybe* in 1973, and a major collection of new and previously published poems, *Stories That Could Be True*, was published in 1977. It was followed by *Smoke's Way* in 1981, *A Glass Face in the Rain* in 1982, *An Oregon Message* in 1987, and *Passwords* in 1991. He has written several other collections of poetry, a fictionalized account of his experiences as a conscientious objector, and is translator, with Aijaz Ahmad and Adrienne Rich, of *Poems by Ghalib*.

In a recent book, *Passwords*, he expresses the hope, in a poem titled "Passwords: A Program of Poems," that his poems might bring strangers—poet and reader—somehow together:[4]

> Might people stumble and wander
> for not knowing the right words,
> and get lost in their wandering?
>
> So—should you stand in the street
> answering all passwords
> day and night for any stranger?
>
> You couldn't do that.
> But sometimes your words
> might link especially to some other person.
>
> Here is a package,
> a program of passwords.
> It is to bring strangers together.

There are people who stumble and wander, who get lost in their wandering because they do not know what they need to know. His poems are designed to bring a few of such wanderers, strangers to one another, together.

SON OF HAWK, SON OF RUBY

A number of Stafford's poems are about his father and mother, and how he was both like and unlike them as a child. In "Parentage," he indicates that his father's brand of heroism is not for him:[5]

> My father didn't really belong in history.
> He kept looking over his shoulder at some mistake.
> He was a stranger to me, for I belong.
>
> There never was a particular he couldn't understand,
> but there were too many in too long a row,
> and like many another he was overwhelmed.
>
> Today drinking coffee I look over the cup
> and want to have the right amount of fear,
> preferring to be saved and not, like him, heroic.

I want to be as afraid as the teeth are big,
I want to be as dumb as the wise are wrong:
I'd just as soon be pushed by events to where I belong.

Not that his father was necessarily foolhardy, a taker of unnecessary risks, for, as "Mouse Night: One of Our Games"[6] reveals, his father could also counsel prudence: On an evening of thunder and developing rain, a field mouse ran for cover, and his father—"my tremendous father"—cowered, observing, "Lions rushing make that sound. . . . Duck and cover: It takes a man to be a mouse this night." Of course, as the title suggests, it was only a game his father was playing. He was not truly afraid. Yet, for the boy, it was a word of caution and warning: There are times that call for heroic deeds, and there are times when it is more manly to duck and take cover. The trick is to discern which is which.

Stafford's phrase in "Parentage"—"the right amount of fear"—is especially telling, as his poems about his mother indicate that she was inordinately fearful, almost immobilized by her fears, and he was determined not to be like her in this respect. "In Fear and Valor"[7] observes that

My mother was afraid
and in my life her fear has hid:
when Perseus holds the Gorgon's head,
she cringes, naked.

Clothed in my body, wild,
even as I grew strong,
my mother, weeping, suffered
the whole world's wrong.

Vanquished and trembling before she died,
she claimed a place in my every limb:
my mother, lost in my stride, fears Death,
as I hunt him.

As his father was a trapper and hunter, there is more of his father in this disposition to hunt Death, to stalk his mortal enemy, though it probably would not have occurred to his father to take on such a formidable foe.

The same theme of his mother's fears appears in "Ruby Was Her Name":[8]

My mother, who opened my eyes, who
brought me into the terrible world,
was guilty. Her look apologized:
she knew what anyone said was true about us
but therefore unfair. How could they blame us
for doing the things we were set to do?

Never heroic, never a model
for us, or for anyone, she cowered
and looked from the corner of her eye—
"Et tu?" And it always meant we were
with her, alas. No one else
could find the center of the world.

She found the truth like a victim; it hit
her again and again, and she always cried out.
At the end she turned to me, helplessly
honest still: "Oh, Bill, I'm afraid,"
and the whole of her life went back to her heart,
from me in a look for the look she gave.

Her way of handling fear was to try to avoid places where possible danger lurked, or to anticipate potential danger and neutralize it in advance. We are given a glimpse of the former strategy in "Vacation Trip":[9]

The loudest sound in our car
was Mother being glum:

Little chiding valves
a surge of detergent oil
all that deep chaos
the relentless accurate fire
the drive shaft wild to arrive

And tugging along behind in its great big
balloon,
that looming piece of her mind:

"I wish I hadn't come."

In "My Mother Was a Soldier,"[10] she advocates a different strategy, that of anticipating potential danger and neutralizing it beforehand:

> If no one moved on order, she would kill—
> that's what the gun meant, soldier. No one
> told you? Her eye went down the barrel; her hand
> held still; gunpowder paid all that it owed
> at once. No need to count the dead.
>
> Hunting, she dragged the bait till nightfall, then
> hung it in a tree and waited. Time
> was working for her, and the quiet. What a world
> it is, for thinkers! Contact would come, and
> the wildest foe fall fastest, Mother said.
>
> Tapping on my wrist, she talked: "Patience
> is the doctor; it says try; it says
> they think we're nice, we quiet ones, we die
> so well: that's how we win, imagining things
> before they happen." "No harm in being quiet,"
>
> My mother said: "that's the sound that finally wins."

Her verbal message is that what one fears is not overcome by taking risks, but by thinking ahead, "imagining things before they happen." This is how one wins in life, by staying ahead of what one fears. Yet there is a deeper message, more ominous, in her actions, one designed to strike fear in her opponent, who happens, in this case, to be her son. By delaying the punishment, she just as surely caused her son to become a "thinker," one who would imagine things before they happened, those feared yet inescapable consequences of failing to move on order. A woman who lived in fear of the outside world knew how to strike fear in her own children.

How to deal with a soldier mother who, in her patient, quiet way, was determined to win at all costs? As a boy, Stafford felt the only thing to do was to placate her. He tells how this worked, or, better, was supposed to work, in "Mother's Day":[11]

> Peg said, "This one," and we bought it
> for Mother, our allowance for weeks
> paid out to a clerk who snickered—

a hideous jar, oil-slick in color,
glass that light got lost in.

We saw it for candy, a sign for
our love. And it lasted:
the old house on Eleventh,
a dim room on Crescent where
the railroad shook the curtains,
that brief glory at Aunt Mabel's place.

Peg thought it got more beautiful,
Egyptian, sort of, a fire-sheened
relic. And with a doomed grasp
we carried our level of aesthetics
with us across Kansas, proclaiming
our sentimental badge.

Now Peg says, "Remember that candy jar?"
She smoothes the silver. "Mother
hated it." I am left standing
alone by the counter, ready to buy what
will hold Mother by its magic, so
she will never be mad at us again.

As he grew older, he realized that placating her would not work, so he adopted another approach, what he calls in "Turn Over Your Hand" that "long silent evasion" that one's life often becomes.[12] Such evasive action is revealed in "Dear Mother,"[13] in which he relates that he is currently engaged in a number of stunning exploits that demand all of his time, their very fancifulness implying that he is looking for excuses for why "I won't be home for a while."

Yet there was something that bound him to her, and, in "A Memorial for My Mother,"[14] he tells her what he believes this was:

For long my life left hers. It went
among strangers; it weakened and followed
foreign ways, even honesty, and courage. It found
those most corrupting of all temptations,
friends—their grace, their faithfulness.

But now my life has come back. In our bleak
little town I taste salt and smoke again.

15

> I turn into our alley and lean
> where I hid from work or from anything
> deserving of praise. Mother, you and I—
>
> We knew if they knew our hearts they would blame.
> We knew we deserved nothing. I go along
> now being no one, and remembering this—
> how alien we were from others, how hard we chewed
> on our town's tough rind. How we loved its flavor.

The muted sarcasm of the first few lines—his "confession" that her prodigal son had gone out into the world and become a person of virtue who also made good and faithful friends—recedes in the final lines into a very different confession, more poignant, less challenging toward her negative view of the world, a remembrance of their shared sense of not belonging to this or any other "bleak little town."

A theme that runs through many of his poems was how his family was not accepted by the townspeople, for reasons that are only obliquely hinted at, but which his mother deeply felt. In "Some Shadows,"[15] he comments on how his mother was ostracized by the neighbors, probably not because they feared the man she had married, but because they looked down upon his manner of earning a living:

> You would not want too reserved a speaker—
> that is a cold way to live.
> But where I come from withdrawal
> is easy to forgive.
>
> When Mother was a girl Indians
> shadowed that country, the barren lands.
> Mother ran to school winter mornings
> with hot potatoes in her hands.
>
> She was like this—foreign, a stranger.
> She could not hear very well;
> the world was all far. (Were the others laughing?
> She never could tell.)
>
> Later, though she was frightened,
> she loved, like everyone.

A lean man, a cruel, took her.
I am his son.

He was called Hawk by the town people,
but was an ordinary man.
He lived by trapping and hunting
wherever the old slough ran.

Our house was always quiet.
Summers the windmill creaked, or a board.
I carried wood, never touching anyone.
Winters the black stove roared.

Forgive me these shadows I cling to, good people,
trying to hold quiet in my prologue.
Hawks cling the barrens wherever I live.
The world says, "Dog eat dog."

Stafford's biography identifies his father, Earl, as a local businessman. But here, in the poem, he is "Hawk," hunter and trapper. Is the poem a little boy's fantasy? Was he embarrassed that his father was a mere businessman, and so he created a father in the image of a hero, a man who put women in their place ("A lean man, a cruel, took her")? This could be. Yet there was something about the Stafford family that prohibited their fitting in, and the reason seems to be that it was this man, nicknamed "Hawk," who represented the family to the world.

In "1932,"[16] Stafford reflects on the rejection that his family experienced from the town when their house was quarantined:

Nobody could come because ours was the house
with the quarantine sign in red, "Scarlet Fever."
We looked out through the tree that whispered all night
its green "Life, life in the world."

Others had school. They would live. They
could run past every day and not look.
At night we listened for stars, and we talked
of miles we would go sometime if our house
let us out, if the doctor ever said yes.

When they took the sign down it was over,
but we carried a lesson the stars had brought,
those times when people turned away.

Underlying his sense of the town's rejection was the even deeper hurt of
knowing that his mother was a victim in life. She talked gamely about
winning, but she knew that her own life, at least, was that of a loser who, by
any objective standard, deserved to lose. If his father went about town with
his head held high, she knew better. "Our Kind" comments on her brutally
honest appraisal of the Staffords:[17]

Our mother knew our worth—
not much. To her, success
was not being noticed at all.
"If we can stay out of jail,"
she said, "God will be proud of us."

"Not worth a row of pins,"
she said, when we looked at the album:
"Grandpa?—ridiculous."
Her hearing was bad, and that
was good: "None of us ever says much."

She sent us forth equipped
for our kind of world, a world of
our betters, in a nation so strong
its greatest claim is no boast,
its leaders telling us all, "Be proud"—

But over their shoulders, God and
our mother, signaling: "Ridiculous."

This insistence against unwarranted self-pride was consistent with her
teaching of an unusual but potentially valuable life strategy: the art of learning
how to lose. In "A Life, a Ritual,"[18] he recalls the strange song she sang of
fortune and success:

My mother had a child, one dark
like her, but bland—wide gaze—who stared
where eternity was, then back to her eyes,

18

and the world. A blanket protected, a song
instructed, and the years came along, came along.

There are people whose game is success, but others
hear distance: guided, often betrayed,
they wander their lives. Their voices go by
every day, outside of history, outside
of importance. They ritual whatever they do.

My mother is nothing now. Her child—
wide gaze like hers—remembers the blanket,
and the song that taught how to lose. Oh, shadow
that came large on a wall, then face that recognized
mine: this distant song about failure

Is for you, is for you.

For her, there was a note of melancholy, perhaps of bitterness, in the song about losing. But, for her son, to accept losing is to accept oneself, to embrace the freedom of being who one really and truly is. In "Learning How to Lose,"[19] he puts it this way:

All your years learning how to live to win,
how others judge you, who counts—you know
it's wrong: but those habits cling that brought you
this freedom. You know how to earn it but
you don't know what it is—a friend that you
make is conquered, like an enemy.

Somewhere you'll rest, have faith, even
lose sometimes, accept the way you are, say
easily to the world: "Leave me alone, Hours.
I'm just living here. Let Now win."

If the lesson his mother taught him was the life strategy of learning to lose, what he learned from his father was the value of attentive listening. He relates in "Listening"[20] how

My father could hear a little animal step,
or a moth in the dark against the screen,

19

and every far sound called the listening out
into places where the rest of us had never been.

More spoke to him from the soft wild night
than came to our porch for us on the wind;
we would watch him look up and his face go keen
till the walls of the world flared, widened.

My father heard so much that we still stand
inviting the quiet by turning the face,
waiting for a time when something in the night
will touch us too from that other place.

If, in his living, his father had taught the value of listening, his death revealed how little he spoke. Stafford laments in "Elegy"[21] the fact that the right words had not been spoken: "If only once in all those years the right goodby could have been said!" He longs for messages from his father, but those that "come spinning back into sound" are as "leaves rustling." Instead, "Come battering. I listen, am the same, waiting."

As the son of Hawk and Ruby, Stafford is aware that their influence was considerable. He is also aware of something in him that wants to use the fact of their influence to explain why his life turned out as it did. In "An Archival Print,"[22] he says, "Now, you want to explain. Your mother was a certain— how to express it?—*influence*. Yes. And your father, whatever he was, you couldn't change that. No." Yet, this is so much talk, and no explanation at all. As God snaps the picture, you can go on like this, talking and talking, but no one is really listening, not even yourself.

Still, if parental influence does not explain his life, or the person he has become, it does have something to do with his sense of vocation. In "Vocation,"[23] he suggests that his calling was forged out of the tension he experienced as the son of this father and this mother:

This dream the world is having about itself
includes a trace on the plains of the Oregon trail,
a groove in the grass my father showed us all
one day while meadowlarks were trying to tell
something better about to happen.

I dreamed the trace to the mountains, over the hills,
and there a girl who belonged wherever she was.

But then my mother called us back to the car:
she was afraid; she always blamed the place,
the time, anything my father planned.

Now both of my parents, the long line through the plain,
the meadowlarks, the sky, the world's whole dream
remain, and I hear him say while I stand between the two,
helpless, both of them part of me:
"Your job is to find what the world is trying to be."

So the parent who goes out into the world, encouraging a certain amount of heroism, is the parent whose voice prevails, and whose appeal for attentive listening in this world will make itself felt in poem after poem. Yet this voice will not have absolute control, as the son has also listened—attentively—to his mother's words and songs, and knows that there is always that passive force in the world which does not want to be anything more than it already is. Here, in the tension between the two forces, the son's vocation is born.

BROTHER BOB AND SISTER PEG

Dust jackets and book covers attest to Stafford's humor and playfulness, and many of his poems blur the distinction between a good poem and a well-told joke. Nothing we have said so far about his parentage would prepare us for this side of his art. To the extent that humor is learned in childhood, often serving as a defense against what is feared, one locus of this learning was surely his relationship to his only brother, Bob, who was five years younger.

Religion was a serious matter in the Stafford household. In "One Home,"[24] Stafford writes: "Plain black hats rode the thought that made our code. We sang hymns in the house; the roof was near God." In light of this, Bob's struggle with religion was the source of comic relief. "Religion Back Home"[25] includes this episode:

When my little brother chanted,
"In 1492 Jesus crossed the ocean blue,"
Mother said, "Bob, you mean
Columbus crossed the ocean blue."
And he said, "I always did get
them two guys mixed up."

In "A Scene in the Country by a Telegraph Line,"[26] their father is struggling to teach them that letters come across the telegraph wires. Their sister doesn't want to learn because it is better that people who want to talk seek face-to-face recognition. Not nearly as principled, Bob is game to learn. But, "Do you hear the letters, Bob?" "Yeah—some."

There is obvious affection between the two brothers, but there is also the pain of realizing, years later, that Bob was vulnerable and needed help, and Bill, for reasons that seemed sound enough at the time, did not come through for his younger brother. "Remembering Brother Bob"[27] was written after Bob's death:

> Tell me, you years I had for my life,
> tell me a day, that day it snowed
> and I played hockey in the cold.
> Bob was seven, then, and I was twelve,
> and strong. The sun went down. I turned
> and Bob was crying on the shore.
>
> Do I remember kindness? Did I
> shield my brother, comfort him?
> Tell me, you years I had for my life.
>
> Yes, I carried him. I took
> him home. But I complained. I see
> the darkness; it comes near: and Bob,
> who is gone now, and the other kids.
> I am the zero in the scene:
> "You said you would be brave," I chided
> him. "I'll not take you again."
> Years, I look at the white across
> this page, and think: I never did.

In "A Game and a Brother,"[28] the two brothers are playing a game of make-believe, apparently to see whether they can make the world—big and fearful—go away. But the older brother, now bereaved, wants to break through the pretending, to remove the mask, and say that he did the best he could: "Bob, it's just me—I tried. I tried." In "At the Grave of My Brother,"[29] he suggests that Bob was beaten by the world, never quite living up to his promise:

The mirror cared less and less at the last, but
the tone of his voice roamed, had more to find,
back to the year he was born; and the world
that saw him awhile again went blind.

Drawn backward along the street, he disappeared
by the cedars that faded a long time ago
near the grave where Mother's hair was a screen
but she was crying. I see a sparrow

Chubby like him, full of promise, barely
holding a branch and ready to fly.
In his house today his children begin
to recede from this year and go their own way.

Brother: Good-bye.

For both, the house in which they grew up was a heavy place, make-believe games and courageous forays into the world providing some relief. But, in the end, Bob was wounded by it, and could never quite find his way to freedom. The house, the town, a sorrowful mother, drew him backward until finally he was gone.

Sister Peg, eighteen months Bill's junior, was a very different kind of victim. In "A Catechism"[30] he asks:

Who challenged my soldier mother?
    Nobody.
Who kept house for her and fended off the world?
    My father.
Who suffered most from her oppressions?
    My sister.
Who went out into the world to right its wrongs?
    My sister.
Who became bitter when the world didn't listen?
    My sister.
Who challenged my soldier sister?
    Nobody.
Who grew up and saw all this and recorded it and
kept wondering how to solve it but couldn't?
    Guess who.

Both women—his mother and his sister—were soldiers, but there is greater sympathy for the woman who did her soldiering at home than for the one who took it out on the world, and then, when the world failed to respond, on herself.

AUNT MABEL

A very different woman from his sister and mother was his Aunt Mabel, a woman who could not be pushed around. In "Aunt Mabel"[31] he recalls his hometown and her presence there:

> This town is haunted by some good deed
> that reappears like a country cousin, or truth
> when language falters these days trying to lie,
> because Aunt Mabel, an old lady gone now, would
> accost even strangers to give bright flowers
> away, quick as a striking snake. It's deeds like this
> have weakened me, shaken by intermittent trust,
> stricken with friendliness.
>
> Our Senator talked like war, and Aunt Mabel
> said, "He's a brilliant man,
> but we didn't elect him that much."
>
> Everyone's resolve weakens toward evening
> or in a flash when a face melds—a stranger's, even—
> reminded for an instant between menace and fear:
> There are Aunt Mabels all over the world,
>   or their graves in the rain.

She was disarming, her words and deeds capable of breaking through a young boy's (if not a town's) defenses, making him a bit trustful, friendly, unafraid. In "A Family Turn,"[32] evidently about the same aunt, he describes her as a woman who would not flinch from truth and told no lies, however harmless they might have seemed. Here, she is armed to the teeth, and the town is her personal battlefield:

> All her Kamikaze friends admired my aunt,
> their leader, charmed in vinegar,

a woman who could blaze with such white blasts
as Lawrence's that lit Arabia.
Her mean opinions bent her hatpins.

We'd take a ride in her old car
that ripped like Sherman through society:
Main Street's oases sheltered no one
when she pulled up at Thirty-first
and whirled that Ford for another charge.

We swept headlines from under rugs, names
all over town, which I learned her way, by heart,
and blazed with love that burns because it's real.
With a turn that's our family's own,
she'd say, "Our town is not the same"—

Pause—"And it's never been."

In contrast to his mother, here is a woman who will not allow the town to break her heart. She will break the town first. In contrast to his mother, the foot soldier, here is a general who orders her troops to take no prisoners. She is a woman who believes there is nothing to fear from this pitiful town, and she will fight it, shot for shot, barb for barb.

CLASSMATES AND NEIGHBORHOOD FRIENDS

Yet the Aunt Mabels of this world belong to the adult world and can only be admired from a respectful distance. She does not take her nephew under her wing, and he learns from her only because he is able to watch and listen. For real community, for a society in which he can know his own tender feelings and the world's tender mercies, there was school, and especially classmates, who seem to exist today much as he remembers them back then. His poems about classmates reveal the tender side of Stafford's self, the boy he describes in "A Touch on Your Sleeve"[33] as a "kind boy" whose disposition was to help others, and whose deepest pain was the realization that most situations are beyond saving. In "Thinking for Berky"[34] he recalls the girl who was beyond saving:

In the late night listening from bed
I have joined the ambulance or the patrol

25

screaming toward some drama, the kind of end
that Berky must have some day, if she isn't dead.

The wildest of all, her father and mother cruel,
farming out there beyond the old stone quarry
where highschool lovers parked their lurching cars,
Berky learned to love in that dark school.

Early her face was turned away from home
toward any hardworking place; but still her soul,
with terrible things to do, was alive, looking out
for the rescue that—surely, some day—would have to come.

Windiest nights, Berky, I have thought for you,
and no matter how lucky I've been I've touched wood.
There are things not solved in our town though tomorrow came:
there are things time passing can never make come true.

We live in an occupied country, misunderstood;
justice will take us millions of intricate moves.
Sirens will hunt down Berky, you survivors in your beds
listening through the night, so far and good.

If Berky had parents who were cruel, there was the girl in "At Liberty School"[35] who had no mother at all. Like Berky, he will not let her out of his mind, though he knows, as he knew then, that the best he could do was to wonder how it was for her:

> Girl in the front row who had no mother
> and went home every day to get supper,
> the class became silent when you left early.
>
> Elaborate histories were in our book
> but of all the races you were the good:
> the taxes of Rome were at your feet.
>
> When the bell rang we did not write any more.
> Traitor to everything else, we poured
> to the fountain. I bent and thought of you.

Our town now is Atlantis, crystal-water-bound;
at the door of the schoolhouse fish are swimming round;
thinking in and out of the church tower go deep waves.

Girl in the front row who had no mother,
as I passed the alleys of our town toward supper
there were not spiteful nails in any board.

Another girl who was beyond saving was "The Girl Engaged to the Boy Who Died."[36] Here was another victim of circumstances outside her control, and a caring observer could only take note of the tragedy of a life that would be spent in unspoken despair:

A part of the wind goes around her face,
and a part still leans where the old wind
came past the radiator cap, and held
the town gently for inspection, for
years, against the cracked windshield.

A part of the room around her chair
holds like that rock at the waterfall
where floods in the park learned
the spring rules; now the trained world,
terrifying, for years, does not
come in to disturb her hair.

A part of her eye waits for a figure
that spun close in the breath she blew
at the birthday candles, and the smoke
for years wandered into corners and waited
while packages crackled in impatient hands.

And the whole sky sprang onto her blue
umbrella she held over her head when she
ran home alone, after graduation, and saw
the yard and the dingy door of her house,
and the weeds in the drive, for years.

If many of his classmates were beyond saving, there were times when this "kind boy" was able to extend a helping hand and offer comforting words. In "One Time"[37] he tells of one such incident:

When evening had flowed between houses
and paused on the schoolground, I met
Hilary's blind little sister following
the gray smooth railing still warm from the sun
with her hand; and she stood by the edge
holding her face upward waiting
while the last light found her cheek
and her hair, and then on over the trees.

You could hear the great sprinkler arm
of water find and then leave the pavement,
and pigeons telling each other their dreams
or the dreams they would have. We were
deep in the well of shadow by then, and I
held out my hand, saying, "Tina, it's me—
Hilary says I should tell you it's dark,
and, oh, Tina, it is. Together now—"

And I reached, our hands touched,
and we found our way home.

There was another time when he saved a girl, only to be rejected, and left now, years later, thinking of the fact that she is no longer alive. In "Dark Wind,"[38] he recalls:

Jean, who no longer is, was
with somebody else. All the air
in the world poured over the lake
that night, warm, and a moon on each
wave as it came. And finally one with a splash
that gasped on the sand, "Save me." I looked
again—it was Jean. I saved her, that once,
who swam back to the dock that night
with somebody else. *I wonder if she got
my letters.* I remember I learned she died,
all the air in the world pouring past.

In "Judgments,"[39] a poem written on the occasion of a class reunion, he is concerned that those who have gone on to do well for themselves—himself included—have done so by fleeing from their childhood struggle against the forces that destroyed the others:

> I accuse—
> Ellen: you have become forty years old,
> and successful, tall, well-groomed,
> gracious, thoughtful, a secretary.
> Ellen, I accuse.
>
> George—
> You know how to help others;
> you manage a school. You never
> let fear or pride or faltering plans
> break your control.
> George, I accuse.
>
> I accuse—
> Tom: you have found a role;
> now you meet all kinds of people
> and let them find the truth of your
> eminence; you need not push.
> Oh, Tom, I do accuse.
>
> Remember—
> The gawky, hardly to survive students
> we were; not one of us going to succeed,
> all of us abjectly aware of how cold,
> unmanageable the real world was?
> I remember. And that fear was true.
> And is true.
>
> Last I accuse—
> Myself: my terrible poise, knowing
> even this, knowing that then we
> sprawled in the world
> and were ourselves part of it; now
> we hold it firmly away with gracious
> gestures (like this of mine!) we've achieved.

I see it all too well—
And I am accused, and I accuse.

He appeals, then, for a certain kind of remembering, or not-forgetting: Let us not forget that the fear was not only in our minds, and thus, irrational, but was a true insight into the nature of the world we live in. We knew cruelty back then (adults often inflicted it), we knew injustice (we were its innocent victims), and we knew untimely death (including deaths that went unnoticed because there was nothing to see, hearts bleeding from pining and rejection). We also knew that we were powerless to save the others or to protect ourselves. Let us not forget who we were: the endangered ones.

The Religious World of Childhood

Stafford grew up in a home, and in towns, where religion was practiced. Though neither parent formally belonged to a church, church was a central part of the social life of small Kansas towns, and the family often attended services together. Several poems about his childhood concern his religious upbringing. His poem "Scripture"[40] suggests that the world the Bible disclosed to him as a boy was dark and shadowy, a land of spirits:

> In the dark book where words crowded together,
> a land with spirits waited, and they rose and walked
> every night when the book opened by candlelight—
>
> A sacred land where the words touched the trees
> and their leaves turned into fire. We carried it wherever
> we went, our hidden scene; and in the sigh of snow coming down,
>
> In the city sometimes a people without any book
> drove tunneling by in traffic, eyes measuring
> chances ahead, the red light at the end of the block—
>
> Then sprung over that city a dark word like judgment
> arched, every face turned into a soul
> wandering the shadow of the tabernacle world.

In "Serving with Gideon,"[41] he draws on the biblical story about Gideon's method for choosing his elite combat force (Judges 7:2–8) to reflect on why he didn't fit in as a boy growing up in small-town Kansas:

Now I remember: in our town the druggist
prescribed Coca-Cola mostly, in tapered
glasses to us, and to the elevator
man in a paper cup, so he could
drink it elsewhere because he was black.

And now I remember The Legion—gambling
in the back room, and no women but girls, old boys
who ran the town. They were generous,
to their sons or the sons of friends.
And of course I was almost one.

I remember winter light closing
its great blue first slowly eastward
along the street, and the dark then, deep
as war, arched over a radio show
called the thirties in the great old U.S.A.

Look down, stars—I was almost
one of the boys. My mother was folding
her handkerchief; the library seethed and sparked;
right and wrong arced; and carefully
I walked with my cup toward the elevator man.

As in the test of Gideon's army, Stafford now realizes that a test of equally cosmic dimensions and tensions was happening here, one involving nothing less than a struggle over a boy's very soul. No wonder that his mother worriedly folded and refolded her handkerchief, and that the library—that font of truth and wisdom in a small town—was not only jumpy and tense, but also profoundly offended that another place in town, the Legion hall, exerted such pressure on a boy who wanted very much to belong. Yet, he passed the test, and the price was that he would never be one of the boys. Instead, he belonged forever to those who belonged to no one, for Gideon's army, unlike the Legion, does not exist outside a story in a book.

In "Back Home"[42] he associates the church with what appears to have been a budding romance which eventually failed:

The girl who used to sing in the choir
would have a slow shadow on dependable walls,
I saw. We walked summer nights.

31

Persons came near in those days,
both afraid but not able to know
anything but a kind of Now.

In the maples an insect sang
insane for hours about how deep the dark was.
Over the river, past the light on the bridge,
and then where the light quelled at limits
in the park, we left the town,
the church lagging pretty far behind.

When I went back I saw many sharp things:
The wild hills coming to drink at the river,
the church pondering its old meanings.
I believe the hills won; I am afraid
the girl who used to sing in the choir
broke into jagged purple glass.

When, years later, he returned and saw the church and recalled the girl who used to sing in the choir, he sensed that he had chosen life beyond the "dependable walls" of the lagging church, and that the girl who sang in the choir was little more than a jagged image, painful to recall.

WHY "THE WANDERER"?

Any number of self-images might have emerged out of the childhood and youth that Stafford experienced. Why, then, does the image of the wanderer come to the fore? Why is it especially compelling to him? The answer lies in the way he understands the image of the wanderer. In "A Life, a Ritual," he identified the people "whose game is success," and then noted that there are others who "hear distance: guided, often betrayed, they wander their lives." As he has described himself as a child "who stared where eternity was," the implication is that he is one of those who, because they hear distance, are most likely to wander off somewhere, far beyond the boundaries of success.

He strikes a similar note in "Existences,"[43] where he depicts himself as a wanderer who is usually gone before the others arrive:

Half-wild, I hear a wolf,
half-tame, I bark. Then

in the dark, I feel my master's
hand, and lick, then bite.

I envy leaves, their touch: miles
by the million, tongues everywhere
saying yea, for the forest,
and in the night, for us.

At caves in the desert, close
to rocks, I wait. I live
by grace of shadows. In moonlight
I hear a room open behind me.

At the last when you come
I am a track in the dust.

Here is a wanderer whose relationship to his master is an ambivalent, unpredictable one: "I feel my master's hand, and lick, then bite." He prefers independence, as he is capable of living on little and needs minimal assistance: "I live by grace of shadows."

In "The Wanderer Awaiting Preferment"[44] he sees himself as one who tries not to request, much less demand, what is his due, recognizing that a wanderer has made a pact with himself that he will take life as it comes:

In a world where no one knows for sure
I hold the blanket for the snow to find:
come winter, then the blizzard, then demand—
the final strategy of right, the snow
like justice over stones like bread.

"Tell us what you deserve," the whole world said.
My hands belong to cold; my voice to dust,
nobody's brother; and with a gray-eyed stare
the towns I pass return me what I give, or claim:
"Wanderer, swerve: but this is a faint command."

Only what the winter gives, I claim. As trees
drink dark through roots for their peculiar grain
while meager justice applauds up through the grass,
I calm the private storm within myself.
Men should not claim, nor should they have to ask.

33

"Only what the winter gives, I claim" portrays a self that does not ask for much, but does claim this much, for winter is about life that is going on below the surface of things, and it is about there being just enough nurturing, down deep, to offer the promise of new life. Winter is also about storms and their calming, and as long as he can calm the private storms within himself, there isn't much point—or need—in asking for the moon.

In "A Message from the Wanderer"[45] he depicts himself standing outside a prison and pointing out to those incarcerated inside that "there are thousands of ways to escape." He tells them how he made his own escape, mainly by looking back and realizing that the means of escape was already in his grasp; he simply hadn't recognized it as such. Then he offers his message:

> Now—these few more words, and then I'm
> gone: Tell everyone just to remember
> their names, and remind others, later, when we
> find each other. Tell the little ones
> to cry and then go to sleep, curled up
> where they can. And if any of us get lost,
> remember: there will come a time when
> all we have said and all we have hoped
> will be all right.

The wanderer goes his own way and toward his own place, but he doesn't fail to leave a message, one that is very simple and deeply reassuring. As we all go out from our prisons, we will need to be able to find one another—hence, the importance of remembering names. As we go out, there is the simple but profoundly important matter of the little ones and who will care for them. They should be allowed to cry if they need to, and encouraged to curl up wherever they can. If anyone gets lost, or cannot go the whole distance, we must remember that a time will come when everything will be all right. So, the wanderer has a message: simple, to the point, and hopeful.

This self-image of the wanderer, and the message it communicates, grows out of Stafford's childhood and his effort to come to terms with it. His life in the Stafford family home, and in the small Kansas towns where he spent his childhood and youth, was very much a prison from which he sought escape. What he learned as he grew older and compared his life with those of his brother and sister is that there are many avenues available to us to make our escape.

The image of the wanderer is also, for Stafford, a way of expressing his caring for others, as he cared for his schoolmates, a caring that does not force the other to accept help on his terms but instead recognizes the other's freedom to respond to his offer of help however the other chooses, or not to respond at all. Conversely, he does not ask for much himself, but is content with what comes his way, as it is never not enough. Such acceptance appears to be a reflection of his mother's acceptance of her lot in life, yet there is less sense of resignation and greater sense that there is great freedom in having and seeking less for oneself. Thus, what the wanderer especially values is his freedom, living his life by grace of shadows. This does not mean that he turns his back on others, or that he cherishes a solitary existence. But he knows that he cannot be comfortable among those who value success over freedom, and who allow themselves to get co-opted by success's demands. Nor does it mean that he is oblivious to the fact that there are those who do not find such freedom, who become lost in their wanderings. Yet even here, he envisions a time, sometime in the future, when it will be possible to look back and affirm what we all—including those who lost their way—have meant to one another.

So, the image of the wanderer reflects Stafford's effort to come to terms with the unfinished business of the past: the father who had certain gifts—especially the capacity to listen for imperceptible sounds—but was not very successful in life, the mother who was afraid of life, the brother who could not free himself from a home and town that kept drawing him backward, and a sister who took her resentment out on the world. Through the self-reflections his vocation as a poet have afforded him, Stafford found a way to break free from the past that continued to imprison his brother and sister. Through this vocation, which required him to struggle with the unfinished business of the past, he realized a margin of freedom from it, which, in turn, allowed him to devote much of his attention to what the world itself is trying to be. This is not to say that he took a rejective stance toward his past, for it is clear that there is much that he continues to value and cherish. Yet, one does not adopt the self-image of "the wanderer" unless one perceives that it was necessary for him to leave home—decisively—even at the risk of losing his way.

One of my favorite Stafford poems is "Fifteen,"[46] a poem that captures the feel of this longing of his to get away:

> South of the bridge on Seventeenth
> I found back of the willows one summer

35

day a motorcycle with engine running
as it lay on its side, ticking over
slowly in the high grass. I was fifteen.

I admired all that pulsing gleam, the
shiny flanks, the demure headlights
fringed where it lay; I led it gently
to the road and stood with that
companion, ready and friendly. I was fifteen.

We could find the end of a road, meet
the sky on out Seventeenth. I thought about
hills, and patting the handle got back a
confident opinion. On the bridge we indulged
a forward feeling, a tremble. I was fifteen.

Thinking, back farther in the grass I found
the owner, just coming to, where he had flipped
over the rail. He had blood on his hand, was pale—
I helped him walk to his machine. He ran his hand
over it, called me good man, roared away.

I stood there, fifteen.

In an autobiographical essay, Stafford noted that the houses in which he grew up were always near the edge of town, beyond which there was "adventure, fields forever, or rivers that wended off over the horizon, forever."[47] The boy in "Fifteen" knows that the motorcycle is a means to indulge his desire for adventure. His disappointment, then, is all the more poignant, as he accepted what had to be accepted, and watched as the motorcycle's owner sped away to places the young Stafford had wanted so much to go. I think, though, that Stafford—the adult reflecting back on this experience—feels a special affection for the boy who demonstrated an uncalculating helpfulness toward the motorcycle's owner, even though it cut across the grain of his deepest desires. It was his nature to be kind.

SELF-IMAGES AND PASTORAL IMAGES

Seminarians are often challenged by their teachers to discover the pastoral image that works best for them. Gaylord Noyce, in *The Minister as Moral*

Counselor, tells us that he has often asked his students to write an essay on the image or metaphor that informs their understanding of ministry: "Students have given me insightful essays on the minister as artist, as exegete, as storyteller, and as historian, integrating the multifarious activities of the pastor around such organizing themes, and following the theme into newly suggested byways of understanding."[48] Noyce himself, after noting recent books that advocate images and models of the minister as politician, prophet, evangelist, and resident theologian, chooses and then elaborates throughout his own book the metaphor of the coach.

In a number of my own writings, I have explored and elaborated on Alastair V. Campbell's suggestion that the three predominant pastoral metaphors in recent years have been the shepherd, the wounded healer, and the wise fool.[49] Like Noyce, I have invited seminarians to explore one or more of these existing images, trying them on for size, or to develop an image of their own creation.

At the other end of the spectrum, seminarians and pastors have been encouraged to take the Myers-Briggs Type Indicator as a means to find out their own personality type. As Gary Harbaugh notes, he has been among those seminary professors who have encouraged the use of the Myers-Briggs. Yet as he himself acknowledges, the Myers-Briggs Type Indicator does not enable one to discover one's unique individuality, one's true self; it only identifies one as a "type." While journaling can be a valuable method for such self-discovery, I have found that seminarians also respond very positively to the invitation to write an autobiography of about twenty-five pages in length, and then to go through the autobiography in search of the self which is there—implicitly—in the text itself. For many, this has been a valuable method of self-discovery. Few of us are accomplished authors; still fewer are gifted poets. But each of us has a unique advantage over all others when it comes to telling the story of our lives: It is *our* story and no one knows it better, more intimately, than we.

Stafford's poetry alerts us to the profound relationship between our early experiences—our childhood and youth—and the unique ways in which we go about our life's vocation. When we go back in memory to our own childhood and youth, as Stafford does in so many of his poems, we discover the unique self that we were, even then, and come to a new appreciation for how our uniqueness came to be formed. We become newly aware of the differences—as well as the similarities—between ourselves and those with whom we have shared life: parents, brothers, sisters, classmates, and others. Within each of us there lives a self which is uniquely our own, and this self is the special gift that we bring to our vocation. Stafford is saying through his poetry that he has faith in this self and trusts it because, after all, it is his primary source of inspiration. And so is the self that we bring to our vocation as pastors.

In "A Ritual to Read to Each Other,"[50] Stafford points out that our failure to know the kind of person we are leads us to follow a pattern that others have made, and in following that pattern, we run the risk of getting lost in the dark and contributing to the darkness experienced by others. The idea that there is safety in conformity to preexisting patterns and models does not apply to the self:

> If you don't know the kind of person I am
> and I don't know the kind of person you are
> a pattern that others made may prevail in the world
> and following the wrong god home we may miss our star.
>
> For there is many a small betrayal in the mind,
> a shrug that lets the fragile sequence break
> sending with shouts the horrible errors of childhood
> storming out to play through the broken dyke.
>
> And as elephants parade holding each elephant's tail,
> but if one wanders the circus won't find the park,
> I call it cruel and maybe the root of all cruelty
> to know what occurs but not recognize the fact.
>
> And so I appeal to a voice, to something shadowy,
> a remote important region in all who talk:
> though we could fool each other, we should consider—
> lest the parade of our mutual life get lost in the dark.
>
> For it is important that awake people be awake,
> or a breaking line may discourage them back to sleep;
> the signals we give—yes or no, or maybe—
> should be clear: the darkness around us is deep.

2. PASTORAL CONVERSATION AS EMBODIED LANGUAGE

GAYLORD NOYCE'S BOOK, *THE ART OF PASTORAL CONVERSATION*, IS CONcerned with improving our pastoral conversations, "the conversations we have as we try to serve our fellow men and women in caring ways."[1] He begins by stressing the significance of conversation, noting that it is "a basic vehicle in human relationships, and the importance of relationships can hardly be overemphasized. Without them human life is impossible. The human self emerges only out of relationship! In no other way can we become persons."[2]

Noyce identifies the four types of conversation in which pastors may, and often, become involved. First is the *turning-point* conversation, where a person is at a junction, trying to make a decision, and somehow a talk helps to clarify the mind and will. Second is a *shared self-disclosure*, where two persons move to a new level of mutual understanding because one or the other reveals more than had been uncovered before. Third is a *growing edge exchange*, where the interests of one person and the competence of another are in such resonance that both learn from the conversation. Fourth is a *rehearsal*, or conversations that enable the participants to share and celebrate and remember certain events. Pastors can and do participate in, and facilitate, each and every one of these types of conversations.[3]

In a chapter titled "The Nondirective Handicap," however, Noyce is concerned that, while the nondirective (or "Rogerian") approach to pastoral care and counseling reveals the inadequacies of pastoral conversation that merely offers advice or religious platitudes, there is the danger that, when this approach is used, the faith that sustains our own ministry will not be communicated to the person in need: "We know our listening is very important. Yet we continue to wish that those with whom we talk in caring exchanges might know more deeply the robust faith of which they are capable."[4] He contends that pastors need to feel free to go beyond the legitimately circumscribed domain of secular counseling and to do more than listen: "At the appropriate time we do share something of our response to the other's story. We tell a story too, in our manner or in the words that come from faith as the two of us together face the dilemmas that oppress the one seeking help."[5] Thus, our speaking does not take the place of listening, but is based on our listening, and is a direct outgrowth of it.

Noyce's phrase, "the art of pastoral conversation," is especially appropriate, because it points to the fact that pastoral conversation is not a science, having systematic methods and principles, but an art, or the ability to make certain desirable things happen that would not happen merely by chance. As poetry is also an art, it is well worth our asking whether poetry may be of assistance to us, especially in helping us to overcome "the nondirective handicap" with which so many of us have operated for so much of our professional lives. If poetry can be of help in this regard, it is unlikely to be by providing the content or material that would be used in the pastor's sharing of the story of faith, for this material would come from the pastor's more direct knowledge and understanding of the Christian faith. But perhaps poetry could be valuable in deepening our understanding of conversation itself, of what true conversation involves and exacts of its participants. Perhaps poetry might also shed light on what listening is all about, because it may be that we have settled for an impoverished understanding of what listening is by allowing it to be defined in the language and terms of "nondirective" counseling.

On the other hand, I do not believe the problem is with Carl Rogers's own approach but with the way it has been trivialized and watered down in its application to pastoral care. The verbatim, a commonly used pedagogical device in pastoral care courses in seminary and in Clinical Pastoral Education, has contributed to such trivialization, as it has given the impression that "nondirective" care and counseling is largely a matter of paraphrasing the parishioner's or client's words, as though one is engaged in a kind of wordplay. Of course, this is not what those who have used the verbatim have intended to communicate or teach, but, all too often, this has been the outcome. It is little wonder, then, that pastoral theologians like Noyce would refer to the nondirective approach developed by Rogers as a "handicap," and that we are now witnessing a strong backlash against the "Rogerian" approach to pastoral care and counseling.

What poetry may enable us to do is to recover those features of Rogers's client-centered approach that were not adequately carried over into pastoral care and counseling when his model was introduced to seminarians and pastors. In this chapter, I will use the poetry of Denise Levertov to show how the nondirective or client-centered approach need not be a handicap to pastors in their pastoral conversations, but a powerful resource. To make this case, I need first to introduce a few selections from Rogers's writings that reveal his own understanding of what transpires between the counselor and the client when the counselor is working out of a nondirective or client-centered orientation.

Two Key Features of Client-Centered Counseling

First, there is Rogers's insistence on the importance of empathy or empathic understanding in the counselor's attitude toward and response to the client. This is also described by Rogers as placing oneself within the internal frame of reference of the client. Here is one of his many efforts to explain what such empathy is and entails:

> The fourth condition for therapy is that the therapist is experiencing an accurate, empathic understanding of the client's world as seen from the inside. To sense the client's private world as if it were your own, but without ever losing the "as if" quality—this is empathy, and this seems essential to therapy. To sense the client's anger, fear, or confusion as if it were your own, yet without your own anger, fear, or confusion getting bound up in it, is the condition we are endeavoring to describe. When the client's world is this clear to the therapist, and he moves about in it freely, then he can both communicate his understanding of what is clearly known to the client and can also voice meanings in the client's experience of which the client is scarcely aware.[6]

Rogers calls this process of "seeing the client's world from inside" an *empathic* as opposed to an *emotional* identification because "the counselor is perceiving the hates and hopes and fears of the client through immersion in an empathic process, but without himself, as counselor, experiencing those hates and hopes and fears."[7]

The words, phrases, and sentences spoken by the counselor are expressive of this empathic immersion in the other's private world. As a visitor within this private inner world, the counselor says to the other what this private world feels like to him or her. The counselor avoids evaluative comments—something we rarely avoid in ordinary conversation—and instead limits himself or herself to words, or phrases, or sentences, that convey how this inner world feels. Frequently, the counselor will, without conscious design or intention, articulate an aspect or feature of this inner world which, thus far, the other has not given expression to, and is perhaps not even yet aware of. As one of Rogers's clients confided to him:

> I'm scarcely conscious of you any more; or perhaps it would be better to say I'm not *self*-conscious of you. I'm not scared of your opinion of me (or at least, the tiny remnants just amuse me) though in a sense I'm much more aware of the fact that you must have one, and I'd be quite genuinely interested in hearing it. And quite undisturbed by it, I think. I'm always interested in what you say, now, and perfectly willing to postpone something I was just going to say in order to listen—and *really* listen—to you. You said a lot of things this time that penetrated so far behind what I said that I had some difficulty in seeing that it was what I really meant. And yet you were right, and in spite of your outstripping me so far, I was interested and stimulated, rather than frightened into retreat. Oh golly, I was frightened once, wasn't I? Right near the beginning, when I said something about being rather better off than most people and you rephrased it so that I looked downright conceited. You scored a bull's eye with that one, as I subsequently realized very clearly indeed, but at the time I ran rapidly in the opposite direction. At one point, you said something about relationships that I couldn't see at all. Yet I had the feeling that it was somehow right, so I just agreed without understanding and went on. . . . A lot of your responses got home with a small shock—particularly the recurrent theme of "labels" and "conformity," and a lot of that you dug out of quite unpromising looking material. But those shocks were pleasant—it was a relief to have the pretense stripped away. I want to get rid of it, but I can't quite manage it myself, so you are just carrying out my own, real wish.[8]

As Rogers points out, the counselor's empathic understanding, reflected in accepting, non-evaluative verbal responses, enables the client to experience greater freedom to recognize and express aspects of his or her inner world that were previously unrecognized or denied. In this way, the client is able to own more and more of this inner world, as less and less of it is walled off and pushed out of conscious awareness.

Second, Rogers makes a considerable point of the fact that in client-centered therapy, it is not just the voice, but the total organism that expresses itself. This being the case, the counselor is as likely to respond to the client's body language as to the client's verbal language. In describing the various stages of the therapeutic process, he notes that there is a point in the process when the client experiences a "physiological loosening" which accompanies the freeing of previously inhibited feelings:

> Moistness in the eyes, tears, sighs, muscular relaxation, are frequently evident. Often there are other physiological concomitants. I would hypothesize that in these moments, had we the measure for it, we would discover improved circulation, improved conductivity of nervous impulses.[9]

He then illustrates this physiological component of the therapeutic process with the following example: The client, a young man, has expressed the wish that his parents would die or disappear. "It's kind of like wanting to wish them away, and wishing they had never been. . . . And I'm so ashamed of myself because then they call me, and off I go—swish! They're somehow still so strong. I don't know. There's some umbilical—I can almost feel it inside me—swish." Here he gestures, plucking himself away by grasping at his navel. When the therapist responds by noting that the client's parents have a hold on his umbilical cord, the client says, "It's funny how real it feels. . . . It's like a burning sensation, kind of, and when they say something that makes me anxious I can feel it right here. . . . It's so hard to define the feeling that I feel there." Rogers observes: "Here he is living subjectively in the feeling of dependence on his parents. Yet it would be most inaccurate to say that he is perceiving it. He is *in* it, experiencing it as a strain on his umbilical cord."[10]

In another case, a young man has been having difficulty getting close to a certain unknown feeling. As he begins to explore it, he senses that it has something to do with the fact that he has been "living so much of my life, and seeing so much of my life in terms of being scared of something." He goes on to tell about how his professional activities are just to give him a little safety and "a little world where I'll be secure, you know." Then his tone changes: "Won't you *let* me have this? I kind of *need* it. I can be so lonely and scared without it." The therapist responds: "'Let me hang on to it because I'd be terribly scared if I didn't!' . . . It's a kind of pleading thing too, isn't it?" The client agrees: "I get a sense of—it's this kind of pleading little boy. It's this gesture of begging." At this point, he puts his hands up as if in prayer, and the therapist comments on this gesture: "You put your hands in kind of a supplication." The client responds: "Yeah, that's right. '*Won't* you do this for me?' kind of. Oh, that's terrible! Who, Me? Beg? . . . That's an emotion I've never felt clearly at all—something I've never been . . . (Pause) . . . I've got such a confusing feeling. One is, it's such a wondrous feeling to have these new things come out of me. It amazes me so much each time, and there's that same feeling, being scared that I've so much of this. (Tears) . . . I just don't know myself. Here's suddenly something I never realized, hadn't any inkling of—that it was some *thing* or *way* I wanted to be."[11]

Rogers comments on the fact that the young man's feeling of pleadingness is who he is at this moment: "Here he is, for a moment, experiencing himself as nothing but a pleading little boy, supplicating, begging, dependent. At that moment he is nothing but his pleadingness, all the way through."[12] Rogers then goes on to note that this is usually how it is with deeply felt emotions: "It is not only dependency that is experienced in this all-out kind of fashion. It may be hurt, or sorrow, or jealousy, or destructive anger, or deep desire, or confidence and pride, or sensitive tenderness, or outgoing love. It may be any of the emotions of which man is capable." Then he adds this startling conclusion: "What I have gradually learned from experiences such as this, is that the individual in such a moment, is coming to *be* what he *is*. When a person has, throughout therapy, experienced in this fashion all the emotions which organismically arise in him, and has experienced them in this knowing and open manner, then he has experienced *himself*, in all the richness that exists within himself. He has become what he is."[13] The client's experiencing *is* the client's true self.

An important outcome of client-centered therapy is that the client has acquired "an increasing trust in his organism." As Rogers notes:

> In choosing what course of action to take in any situation, many people rely upon guiding principles, upon a code of action laid down by some group or institution, upon the judgment of others (from wife and friends to Emily Post), or upon the way they have behaved in some similar past situation. Yet as I observe the clients whose experiences in living have taught me so much, I find that increasingly such individuals are able to trust their total organismic reaction to a new situation because they discover to an ever-increasing degree that if they are open to their experience, doing what "feels right" proves to be a competent and trustworthy guide to behavior which is truly satisfying.[14]

Unfortunately, and, I believe, quite unintentionally, the verbatim form which is widely used in the training of seminarians and beginning pastors leads to a view of pastoral conversation as disembodied speech. Little if any attention is paid to the "total organismic context" in which words are spoken and have their essential meaning. What results is a form of Gnosticism in which words are separated from bodies and become like disembodied spirits, floating in air, just out of reach.

I believe that we can recover the spirit of the nondirective or client- centered approach for pastoral conversation by attending to how poets exhibit empathic understanding in their work and locate language in the body, or the total organismic experience. In making this plea—hands in supplication—for this recovery of client-centered emphases, I am not advocating that pastoral counseling per se be client-centered. As I have argued in other writings, I favor a more directive approach to pastoral counseling, especially in the parish setting, owing largely to the time limitations under which parish ministers must work.[15] But, perhaps paradoxically, I think it is altogether possible for pastors to assume the client-centered approach when engaged in the less structured and formal "pastoral conversations" which Noyce has in mind—that is, when pastors are involved in one or another of the four types of conversation which he identifies for us. It is precisely in these more informal, unstructured conversations that the pastor may enter into the inner world of the other with empathic understanding, and may be especially aware of the total organismic experiencing of the other. This is possible because, as Rogers points out, the client-centered approach was originally called "nondirective" because the counselor did not have a predetermined goal in mind nor a predetermined time frame within which this goal was to be reached. Thus, the informal pastoral conversation is the ideal context for the client-centered approach, as it allows for the possibility that any one of Noyce's four types of conversations may emerge in the natural course of conversation. If there is no predetermined goal, and no predetermined time frame for achieving this goal, neither has the type of conversation been decided upon in advance—at least, not by the pastor, who comes, literally, with open arms, open mind, and open heart.

EMPATHIC UNDERSTANDING

Before we review poems by Denise Levertov that bear on our preceding discussion, we need to know something about her and her work. She was born in Ilford, Essex, England, in 1923. Her father was a Russian Jew who converted to Christianity, became an Anglican priest, and dedicated his life to the unification of Christianity and Judaism. Her mother was Welsh. In "Illustrious Ancestors,"[16] Levertov pays homage to a rabbi on her father's side who understood the language of birds because he "listened well, and as it was said, 'prayed with the bench and the floor,' " and to a tailor and preacher on her mother's side "whose meditations were sewn into coats and britches." She was educated by her parents, who saw that she grew up surrounded by books, and never formally schooled. She began writing as a child and at twelve sent some of her poems to T. S. Eliot, who responded with a long letter of advice. Her first volume of poetry, *The Double Image,* published in 1946, was written during World War II, more than three years of which were spent as a hospital nurse at St. Luke's Hospital in London. In 1947 she married an American soldier, the novelist Mitchell Goodman, and in 1948 she moved to New York City, where she gave birth to a son, Nikolai, in 1949. She became a naturalized citizen in 1955.

Her second volume of poetry, *Here and Now,* published in 1956, reflects the major life changes she experienced in the years since the war, and a new understanding of the poetic art itself. While she had encountered disease, poverty, and death as a nurse during the war, the immediacy of these experiences is missing in *The Double Image,* and the poems, written in traditional metrical and stanzaic patterns, tend to start from abstractions, which are then fleshed out with generalized natural images of waves or leaves or stones. According to Carolyn Matalene, "Such vague seeing has never since been characteristic of her poetry, nor does she usually proceed from abstractions."[17] Matalene draws attention to a poem written in 1948 entitled "Too Easy: to Write of Miracles,"[18] which seems to reject Levertov's previous voice, finding that it is "Easy like the willow to lament," but

> difficult to write
> of the real image, real hand, the heart
> of day or autumn beating steadily:
> to speak of human gestures, clarify
> all the context of a simple phrase
> —the hour, the shadow, the fire,
> the loaf on a bare table.

In this period, she "learned to discover poetry in the intense perception of the immediate."[19]

In the early 1960s Levertov began teaching poetry. She has been writer-in-residence or visiting professor at City University of New York, Vassar College, Drew University, University of California at Berkeley, and Massachusetts Institute of Technology, and was for six years professor of English at Tufts University. In 1981 she became professor of English at Stanford University. She has written over forty books of poetry, some of which have been reissued in three major collections comprising poems written during 1940–1960, 1960–1967, and 1968–1972. Her recent books include *The Freeing of the Dust* (1972), *Life in the Forest* (1978), *Candles in Babylon* (1982), *Oblique Prayers* (1984), *Breathing the Water* (1988), *A Door in the Hive* (1989), and *Evening Train* (1992). She has also written books on the poet's craft and the work of other poets and writers, including *The Poet in the World* (1973), *Light Up the Cave* (1981), and *New and Selected Essays* (1992). She resides in Seattle.

During the 1960s she became actively involved in the antiwar movement, and subsequently she has written poems supportive of liberation movements in South and Central America, and against the Persian Gulf War. As Matalene points out, "Her sense of the moral necessity of opposing a war she believed unjust is surely related to her personal history. . . . Her parents, as prisoners of war, were under house arrest in Leipzig during World War I. During World War II, their house was a center for the reception and relocation of Jewish refugees from Hitler. It is hardly likely that of all poets Denise Levertov would have chosen to ignore the political and social issues of the 1960s."[20] On the other hand, to read her poetry as political statement only is to misread it, for, as Diane Wakoski notes, she "has actually been writing a poetry of religious vision, one which comes out of American mysticism. It is a vision which allows Levertov to move beyond her politics, her Judaeo-Christian morality, and most of all, her Romantic fear of the darkness, to a vision that portrays darkness as the other half of light."[21]

To me, one of the most impressive things about Denise Levertov's poetry is her ability to enter the private, inner world of another and express—in words—what the other is experiencing. In "Despair"[22] she observes a woman who, like her, is mourning a loss:

> While we were visiting David's grave
> I saw at a little distance
>
> a woman hurrying towards another grave
> hands outstretched, stumbling
>
> in her haste; who then
> fell at the stone she made for
>
> and lay sprawled upon it, sobbing,
> sobbing and crying out to it.
>
> She was neatly dressed in a pale coat
> and seemed neither old nor young.

I couldn't see her face, and my friends
seemed not to know she was there.

Not to distress them, I said nothing.
But she was not an apparition.

And when we walked
back to the car in silence

I looked stealthily back and saw she rose
and quieted herself and began slowly

to back away from the grave.
Unlike David, who lives

in our lives, it seemed
whoever she mourned dwelt

there, in the field, under stone.
It seemed the woman

believed whom she loved heard her,
heard her wailing, observed

the nakedness of her anguish,
and would not speak.

In "The Old Adam"[23] she focuses her attention on another despairing soul, this one an old man whose life was misspent because he did not get his priorities straight:

A photo of someone else's childhood,
a garden in another country—world
he had no part in and has no power to imagine:

yet the old man who has failed his memory
keens over the picture—"Them happy days—
gone—gone for ever!"—glad for a moment to suppose

a focus for unspent grieving, his floating
sense of loss.
He wanders

asking the day of the week, the time,
over and over the wrong questions.
Missing his way in the streets

he acts out
the bent of his life,
the lost way

never looked for, life
unlived, of which he is dying
very slowly.

"A man,"
says his son, "who never
made a right move in all his life." A man

who thought the dollar was sweet and
couldn't make a buck, riding the subway
year after year to untasted sweetness,

loving his sons obscurely, incurious
who they were, these men, his sons—
a shadow of love, for love longs

to know the beloved, and a light goes with it
into the dark mineshafts of feeling . . . A man
who now, without knowing,

in endless concern for the smallest certainties,
looking again and again at a paid bill,
inquiring again and again, "When was I here last?"

asks what it's too late to ask:
"Where is my life? Where is my life?
What have I done with my life?"

The tone of this poem is not condemnatory—she lets the man's son render the harsh judgment that he "never made a right move in all his life"—but she is not merely sympathetic either, for this would be to ignore how tight and thoughtlessly he lived his life, as reflected now in his confused preoccupation with the "smallest certainties."

In "A Solitude"[24] she tells about her encounter with a blind man who accepts her offer of help. Here her empathy is expressed in her realization that while he accepted her offer of assistance he also prized his capacity to be alone:

A blind man. I can stare at him
ashamed, shameless. Or does he know it?
No, he is in a great solitude.

O, strange joy,
to gaze my fill at a stranger's face.
No, my thirst is greater than before.

In his world he is speaking
almost aloud. His lips move.
Anxiety plays about them. And now joy

of some sort trembles into a smile.
A breeze I can't feel
crosses that face as if it crossed water.

The train moves uptown, pulls in and
pulls out of the local stops. Within its loud
jarring movement a quiet,

the quiet of people not speaking,
some of them eyeing the blind man,
only a moment though, not thirsty like me,

and within that quiet his
different quiet, not quiet at all, a tumult
of images, but what are his images,

he is blind? He doesn't care
that he looks strange, showing
his thoughts on his face like designs of light

flickering on water, for he doesn't know
what look is.
I see he has never seen.

And now he rises, he stands at the door ready,
knowing his station is next. Was he counting?
No, that was not his need.

When he gets out I get out.
"Can I help you towards the exit?"
"Oh, alright." An indifference.

But instantly, even as he speaks,
even as I hear indifference, his hand
goes out, waiting for me to take it,

and now we hold hands like children.
His hand is warm and not sweaty,
the grip firm, it feels good.

And when we have passed through the turnstile,
he going first, his hand at once
waits for mine again.

"Here are the steps. And here we turn
to the right. More stairs now." We go
up into sunlight. He feels that,

the soft air. "A nice day,
isn't it?" says the blind man. Solitude
walks with me, walks

beside me, he is not with me, he continues
his thoughts alone. But his hand and mine
know one another,

it's as if my hand were gone forth
on its own journey. I see him
across the street, the blind man,

and now he says he can find his way. He knows
where he is going, it is nowhere, it is filled
with presences. He says, **I am.**

She is able to enter the man's internal frame of reference by sensing the emotional meaning behind his words, the indifference that lies behind his acceptance of help—"Oh, alright"—and the desire to be alone in his own "great solitude" which expresses itself in his seemingly meaningless observation, "A nice day, isn't it?" In entering his frame of reference, she abandons her own, which was to be more helpful to him than the others on the train who were "not thirsty like me." Yet through this self-abandonment something unanticipated and unplanned occurs, as they find themselves holding hands "like children," and "his hand and mine know one another." Something has happened, wordlessly, between them, and it is far more important than her initial desire to be of assistance to a man who "has never seen."

In "Poet and Person"[25] she elaborates on the theme of her willingness to give of herself versus the other's disposition to settle, finally, for less:

> I send my messages ahead of me.
> You read them, they speak to you
> in siren tongues, ears of flame
> spring from your heads to take them.
>
> When I arrive, you love me,
> for I sing those messages you've
> learned by heart, and bring,
> as housegifts, new ones. You hear
>
> yourselves in them,
> self after self. Your solitudes
> utter their runes, your own
> voices begin to rise in your throats.
>
> But soon you love me less.
> I brought with me
> too much, too many laden coffers,
> the panoply of residence,
>
> improper to a visit.
> Silks and furs, my enormous wings,
> my crutches, and my spare crutches,
> my desire to please, and worse—
>
> my desire to judge what is right.
>
> I take up
> so much space.
> You are living on what you can find,
> you don't want charity, and you can't
> support lingering guests.
>
> When I leave, I leave
> alone, as I came.

She recognizes what every caregiver learns, sooner or later, that there are limits to another's acceptance of one's empathic understanding. Even when she manages to suspend the desire to please and to judge, the other has his or her limits, and it is altogether likely that at some point in the relationship the caregiver will be asked to go.

In "A Wanderer,"[26] a friend is unable to share his grief with her, but seeks out strangers instead:

i

The iris hazel, pupils
large in their round blackness,
his eyes
do see me,
he hugs me
tightly, but

he turns away,
he takes his grief
home with him,
my half of it
hides behind me as I
wave, he waves,
and it and I
close my door for the night.

ii

He has taken his sorrow
away to strangers.
They form a circle around it,
listening, touching,
drawing it forth.

It weeps among them,
begins to shed
cloaks and shawls, its old
gray and threadbare twisted bandages,
and show
pale skin, dark wounds.

My arms are empty,
my warm bed's empty,
I say no
to the lovers who want to warm themselves
in me.
　　　I want

to lie alone, dreaming awhile
about that ring dance,
that round
I don't know how to sing,
that language
strangers talk to him in,
speaking runes to his sorrow.

In "The Mourner"[27] the grieving one's desire is not for consolation by the living but to bear the body and hear the voice of the dead:

Instead of arms to hold you
I want longer limbs, vines,
to wrap you twofold, threefold.

I wrap you, I pick you up, I carry you,
your knees drawn up, your head bent,
your arms crossed on your breast.

You are heavy.
I walk, I walk.
You say nothing.

Onward. Hill and dale. Indoors.
Out again. You say nothing.
You grow smaller, I wrap you fourfold.

I show you all the wonders you showed me,
infinitesimal and immense.
You grow smaller, smaller,
and always heavier. Why will you not speak?

Still Levertov understands that her task is to listen to the pain of others, whether verbalized or not. In "Vocation"[28] she describes herself as one who looks "with the eyes and ears concealed within me":

I have been listening, years now,
to last breaths—martyrs dying
passionately
   in open blood,
   in closed cells:

to screams and surprised silence
of children torn from green grass
into the foul bite
    of the great mower.

From a long way off
I listen, I look
with the eyes and ears concealed within me.
Ears and eyes of my body
know as I know:
I have no vocation to join the nameless great,

only to say to others, Watch! Hear them!
Through them alone
we keep our title, *human,*

word like an archway, a bridge, an altar.
(Sworn enemies
answering phrase to phrase
used to sing in the same key, imagine!—
used to pick up the furious song and
sing it through
to the tonic resting place, the chord,
however harsh,
of resolution.)

Nowadays
I begin to hear a new sound:
a leaf seems as it slowly
twirls down
earthward
  to hum,

55

a candle, silently
melting beneath its flame,
seems to implore
attention, that it not burn its life
unseen.

LISTENING TO THE LANGUAGE OF THE BODY

In each of the foregoing poems, Levertov's empathic understanding of the other is reflected in her awareness of the total organismic context in which feeling or emotion is expressed. She takes particular note of the body language and how it communicates what the other is experiencing emotionally. In "Despair" she notices the woman hurrying toward another grave with "hands outstretched, stumbling in her haste; who then fell at the stone she made for and lay sprawled upon it." In "The Old Adam" she observes the old man "keening" over a photo of someone else's childhood. In "A Solitude" she notes how the blind man's lips move as "in his world he is speaking almost aloud." In "A Wanderer" her own arms express her desire to embrace the feelings of the other, and in "The Mourner" she says she wants "longer limbs," like vines, that could wrap the other, fourfold. These bodily images, especially her emphasis on the hands and arms, bring home the fact that it is not just the voice but the total organism that expresses itself. Her poetry is deeply attuned to the language of the body, and her own body is a source and means of understanding, as in "Vocation": "I look with the eyes and ears concealed within me. Ears and eyes of my body know as I know."

In "She wept, and the women consoled her,"[29] a woman experiences the pain of her grief in every part of her body:

The flow of tears ebbed,
her blouse began to dry.
But the sobs that
took her by the shoulders and
shook her came back
for unknown reasons
and shook her again, like soldiers
coming back when everyone had gone.
History's traffic had speeded up and
smashed into gridlock all around her;
the women consoled her but she couldn't get out.

> Bent forward as she was,
> she found herself looking at her legs.
> They were old, the skin
> shiny over swollen ankles,
> and blotched. They meant nothing to her
> but they were all she could see.
> Her fallen tears had left their traces
> like snail-tracks on them.

They consoled her "but she couldn't get out"—there is no escaping the body and its agonies. Her eyes see nothing but her swollen extremities.

In "The Blue Rim of Memory"[30] bones are exposed to the stabs and pangs of sorrow. They are the locus of the spirit's desolation!

> The way sorrow enters the bone
> is with stabs and hoverings.
> From a torn page
> a cabriolet
> approaches over the crest of a hill,
> first the nodding, straining head of the horse
> then the blind lamps, peering;
>
> the ladies within the insect eagerly
> look from side to side awaiting the vista—
> and quick as a knife
> are vanished. Who were they? Where is the hill?
>
> Or from stoked fires of nevermore
> a warmth constant as breathing hovers out
> to surround you, a cloud of mist
> becomes rain, becomes cloak, then skin.
>
> The way sorrow enters the bone
> is the way fish sink through dense lakes
> raising smoke from the depth
> and flashing sideways in bevelled
> syncopations.
> It's the way the snow
> drains the light from day but then,
> covering boundaries of road and sidewalk,

> widens wondering streets
> and stains the sky yellow
> to glow at midnight.

If every part of the body is object and victim of pain, it is the heart that is most in danger of being overwhelmed by the pain. Yet in "The Heart,"[31] Levertov is impressed by the heart's resilience:

> At any moment the heart
> breaks for nothing—
>
> poor folk got up in their best,
> rich ones trying, trying to please—
>
> each touch and a new fissure appears,
> such a network, I think of an old
> china pie-plate
> left too long in the oven.
>
> If on the bloody muscle its namesake
> patiently pumping in the thoracic cavity
>
> each flick of fate incised itself,
> who'd live long?—but this beats on
>
> in the habit of minute response,
> with no gift for the absolute.
>
> Disasters
> of history weigh on it, anguish
>
> of mortality presses
> in on its sides
>
> but neither crush it to dust nor
> split it apart. What
>
> is under the cracked glaze?

In "Joie de Vivre"[32] she again focuses on the heart, noting how it keeps stalwart and strong as hurts it has sustained in the past return in new guises:

All that once hurt
(healed) goes on hurting
in new ways. One same heart
—not a transplant—
cut down to the stump
throbs, new, old.
Bring paper and pencil
out of the dimlit into
the brightlit room, make sure
all you say is true.
"Antonio, Antonio,
the old wound's
bleeding." "Let it bleed."
The pulse of life-pain
strong again, count it,
fast but
not fluttering.

In a recent poem entitled "Time for Rivets,"[33] she revisits her poem "The Heart," written two decades earlier, and asks whether she was too sanguine about its ability to withstand breaking (maybe tape or rivets are needed?):

Reinforced though it was
with stoic strapping,
my heart was breaking again. Damn!
Just when I had so much to do,
a list as long as your arm.
The world news slithered
toward the probable worst
of a lifetime's bad news,
and as for me (as if in that shadow it mattered—
but it did) in two days' time
I'd be saying goodbye to someone I thought of
"day and night," as I'd not been planning to think
of anyone ever again.

I'd believed it would hold, yes,
I'd considered my serviceable heart
long-since well-mended,

and equal to what demands
might still confront it.
And hadn't I written, still longer ago,
that these metaphorical hearts, although
they "break for nothing," do so
in surface fissures only, a web
of hairline fractures, the way
old pieplates do, rimmed with a blue design
as if someone had pressed them all round
with tines of a fork well-dipped in indigo?

All true enough, but surely by now
mine, though made like such plates
for use, not show, must need
those clamps of metal with which
cracked vessels of finer porcelain are held.
For the moment I'd have to make do
with tape and crossed fingers.

Another recent poem, "Broken Pact,"[34] tells how her heart's desire has weakened her body over the years, leaving mind and heart to figure out how to proceed without the body's active participation:

A face ages quicker than a mind.

And thighs, arms, breasts,
take on an air of indifference.
Heart's desire has wearied them, they chose to forget
whatever they once promised.

But mind and heart continue
their eager conversation,
they argue, they share epiphanies,
sometimes all night they raise
antiphonal laments.

Face and body have betrayed them,

they are alone together,
unsure how to proceed.

The heart, then, is a powerful metaphor for Levertov for the spirit that lives in and through the body. To listen to the language of the body is to listen, above all, to the heart and its desires. If it often overreaches, demanding more than the rest of the body can commit to, it is, nevertheless, the body's spark of life, its source of courage.

While emphasizing the heart as expressive of the body's desires, she also pays close attention to the way the hands speak for the body. We saw this in her poem on the blind man who, in spite of his indifference to her offer of assistance, reached out and took her hand in his. In "Inheritance"[35] she observes that another woman's memory of kind and gentle hands becomes her own, soothing her as well:

> Even in her nineties she recalled
> the smooth hands of the village woman
> who sometimes came from down the street
> and gently, with the softest
> of soft old flannel,
> soaped and rinsed and dried
> her grubby face, while upstairs
> the stepmother lay abed bitterly sleeping,
> the uncorked opiate bottle
> wafting out sticky sweetness
> into a noontime dusk.
> Those hands, that slow refreshment,
> were so kind, I too,
> another lifetime beyond them,
> shall carry towards my death
> their memory,
> grateful, and longing
> once again to feel them soothe me.

In the carrying and giving birth to her own child, a woman becomes highly sensitized to the workings of her own body. If Levertov's poetry went through a transformation in the decade between her first and second volumes—less abstract, more immediate—one likely reason for this was that she gave birth to a son. "Who He Was," written in 1949, centers on the child who was nine months in her body:[36]

One is already here whose life
bearing like seed its distant death, shall grow
through human pain, human joy, shall know
music and weeping, only because
the strange flower of your thighs
bloomed in my body. From our joy
begins a stranger's history. Who
is this rider in the dark? We lie
in candlelight; the child's quick unseen movements
jerk my belly under your hand. Who,
conceived in joy, in joy,
lies nine months alone in a walled silence?

Who is this rider in the dark,
nine months the body's tyrant,
nine months alone in a walled silence
our minds cannot fathom?
Who is it will come out of the dark,
whose cries demand our mercy, tyrant
no longer, but alone still, in a solitude
memory cannot reach?
Whose lips will suckle at these breasts,
thirsting, unafraid, for life?
Whose eyes will look out of that solitude?

The wise face of the unborn
ancient and innocent
must change to infant ignorance
before we see it, irrevocable third
looking into our lives; the child
must hunger, sleep, cry, gaze, long weeks
before it learns of laughter. Love can never
wish a life no darkness; but may love
be constant in the life our love has made.

This poem speaks of her body and his, and of what he will experience when he
comes out of the dark, the "nine months alone in a walled silence our minds
cannot fathom."

Nineteen years later, in "He-Who-Came-Forth," she wrote again of her son, and of how the one who grew in her is now "out in the world beyond my skin":[37]

> Somehow nineteen years ago
>   clumsily passionate
> I drew into me the seed
> of a man—
>   and bore it, cast it out—
>
> man-seed that grew
>   and became a person
>   whose subtle mind and quick heart
>
>   though I beat him, hurt him,
>   while I fed him, loved him,
>
> now stand beyond me, out in the world
>   beyond my skin
>
>   beautiful and strange as if
>   I had given birth to a tree.

Being one who listens, then, involves, for Levertov, hearing the body language of the other, feeling the other's confusion, anguish, pain, and struggle through her own bodily senses—"The eyes and ears of my body." The body of the other speaks when the words are not there, or slow to come. So, in a very real sense, her poetry puts words in the mouths of the silent and speechless, giving voice to what their bodies are silently saying. The reader of her poems could make the mistake of assuming that it is the subject of the poem who is doing the speaking when, more often than not, it is the poet who is finding words to convey what the body is wordlessly saying.

In the poem "She wept, and the women consoled her," the poet speaks for the body by means of metaphors that capture the sobbing woman's pain. There is the metaphor of the soldiers, reminiscent of Vietnam, who returned to the bombed-out village after the inhabitants had fled, and there is the metaphor of history's traffic having speeded up and "smashed into gridlock" all around her. There is nothing tender or wistful in these images. They are harsh images of a metallic, concussive, violent reality. They tell us that the woman's whole being has been senselessly attacked, and that she was and is without defenses, reduced to tearless sobs, and utterly inconsolable.

In "The Blue Rim of Memory" the metaphors are not as violent and unrelenting, but instead promise a certain way out. Here the way sorrow enters the bone "is the way fish sink through dense lakes" and "the way the snow drains the light." While they do not minimize the capacity of sorrow to depress and deplete the soul, these images also envision a way out. Unlike an obliterated village, or gridlocked traffic from which there is no escape, the fish is able to flash "sideways in bevelled syncopations" and the snow appears to widen "wondering streets" and to cause the sky to glow at midnight. Here there is the anticipation of the knife of sorrow being at last withdrawn, of new skin growing over old wounds, as "a warmth constant as breathing hovers out to surround you."

Levertov's poems on various ways the body speaks in the soul's behalf suggest that the pastor's role, as empathic listener, is to leave the realm of abstract and disembodied spirits to others, and to enter the body's world, a world where a woman, bent forward, finds herself looking at her legs, "the skin shiny over swollen ankles, and blotched." When one participates in the body's world, the very form of the communication changes, and something new and different occurs. The *type* of communication may be the same, whether concerned with turning-points, self-disclosure, growing edges, or rehearsal, but its *tone* is very different, as the embodied quality of the conversation is recognized and raised to consciousness.

In illustrating the "turning point" conversation, Noyce tells about a time when he was making a decision about a job—whether to move or to stay where he was. The need to make this decision was beginning to wear on him, as it was a hard decision: "Somehow when decisions come hard, I am tempted to think that one way is 'right' and the other way is 'wrong,' and more and more I fear that my choice might be the latter. Paralysis sets in and the decision gets even harder to make." In this instance, when he was slipping into such a paralysis, a friend said simply, "You'll be happy either way." Noyce says that his friend's words were timely and never forgotten: "It was like a word of grace, lifting a hidden burden from my shoulders."[38]

Note, here, his use of embodied language: The decision is "paralyzing," and, in marked contrast, his friend's words lift "a hidden burden from my shoulders." No doubt the conversation between them had focused on the losses and gains that would result from staying put and from moving on, and no doubt such conversation had been clarifying, helpful to him in arriving at his final decision. But what especially comes through in his recounting of the conversation is the body language he uses to communicate to us both how the decision was wearing on him and how his friend's simple intervention brought such relief.

The friend in this case is like the pastor whom Levertov depicts in her poem "A Cure of Souls":[39]

> The pastor
> of grief and dreams
>
> guides his flock towards
> the next field
>
> with all his care.
> He has heard
>
> the bell tolling
> but the sheep
>
> are hungry and need
> the grass, today and
>
> every day. Beautiful
> his patience, his long
>
> shadow, the rippling
> sound of the flock moving
>
> along the valley.

When a pastor intervenes as Noyce's friend did—helping to release the body from its paralysis and burden—he or she addresses our need for another field in which to satisfy the hunger of our hearts. How "beautiful is the rippling sound of the flock moving along the valley."

THE NONDIRECTIVE HANDICAP

This brings us back, full circle, to the nondirective handicap. Given the way that Rogerian listening has typically been taught and learned, the impression most pastors have of the nondirective approach is that it is largely a matter of paraphrasing the words of the other. The image that comes to mind is that of the pastor as a sort of walking thesaurus. The patient says she is afraid of death, and the pastor says "You feel frightened," or "You are apprehensive," or "You are terrified," or even, "It's kind of scary, isn't it?" These are all synonyms of "afraid." But, as we have seen, empathic understanding of and listening for the language of the body entails much more—and much less—than this walking thesaurus image implies. When our minds take over, when they begin to work apart from and in alienation from our bodies, then we will resort to paraphrasing, to speaking the first synonym for "afraid of death" that enters, unmediated by the body, into our minds.

In embodied listening, it works very differently. When the other says, "I'm afraid of death," this saying is received bodily by the listener, and whatever the listener says, or does not say, by way of response, incorporates the visceral impact of these words upon the listener. In this sense, the listener responds with her own body language. Maybe the words that come forth are, in fact, words like "frightening," "apprehensive," "terrifying," or "scary," as these may well register what the listener has felt in the pit of her own stomach. But, the words, "I'm afraid of death," might also evoke in the listener an internal scream, a hot flash of anger, or a deflated feeling, a felt sense of how overpowering death is. No one expects that words as true and right as poetry will come forth, for, after all, the poet has the luxury—if we may call it that—of having spent days, even weeks or months, trying to find just the right word or phrase to convey what she has felt or is feeling now. But we can accustom ourselves to speaking from our own felt bodily sense of things, and to take notice of the body language of the other: "I notice that your hand is trembling" is likely to speak more truly than "It's kind of scary, isn't it?"

One of Carl Rogers's early associates, Eugene Gendlin, has written a popular book about how we can teach ourselves to listen to our own bodies, to become aware of our total organismic processing. Following Rogers, he talks about a "felt sense" that is different from perception and intuition: "A felt sense is the body's sense of a problem, or of some concern or situation. It is a physical sense of meaning."[40] In Gendlin's view, we can teach ourselves to become attentive to our own felt bodily sense and to articulate, with a high degree of accuracy, how we are experiencing this felt bodily sense at any given time or in any given situation. In pastoral conversations, it is especially useful and valuable if we are able to discriminate between the direct influence of our conversation partner's words and presence on our felt bodily sense, and other factors that are having an effect on our felt bodily sense, including factors in the immediate environment and ones that we brought with us to the present conversation, but which have little or nothing directly to do with it. Those of us who have had the opportunity to watch videotapes of Carl Rogers's counseling sessions have come away enormously impressed with his capacity to screen these extraneous factors and influences out, and to attend with his whole body to what the client is experiencing at that moment. James E. Dittes comments:

> What is the therapeutic power of Carl Rogers, and how is it achieved? What selfhood does he portray in a "client-centered" therapeutic hour? The caricatures are right, or half-right: He seems a nonentity, mechanically parroting the client, bland. The things that we usually suppose make for personality and a sense of self-presence are absent—sociability, opinions and attitudes, feelings and history. Watching him on film or in person, one had a sure sense that, if interrupted during a therapy hour and asked his name, he couldn't answer easily, so radically other-directed was this "non-directive" therapist, so totally abdicating of his distinctiveness and so engrossed in the other, so oblivious to the boundaries that construct and define the self. . . . But there is also a powerful sense of presence. A client, or an observer, has no doubt about having experienced an indelible personality, one who is decisively other even while— or because—strangely merged. Rogers emerges with a raw selfhood, an intense, primitive, generic presence, a kind of ahistorical, asocial, arelational selfhood in a world that is used to defining selfhood in historical, social, relational terms.[41]

The point, of course, is not that we should all become imitators of Carl Rogers. Rather, what this description of Rogers's "presence" suggests to me is that there is, in fact, more of a connection than we might have thought between the listening phase of the pastoral conversation and the phase in which the pastor responds, in manner or in words, with the story that arises from faith. This understanding of listening as an act of self-abnegation is inherently Christian, as it recapitulates the self-emptying with which we associate the Son of God. It also reenacts the rite of Holy Communion, in which we relegate our minds to a secondary status, and, thus having emptied ourselves, take the body of the Other into our own bodies, so that when we speak—as we surely will—we speak the more primitive or primal language of the body's world.

THE HOSPITAL AND THE BODY'S WORLD

In light of our emphasis on learning to participate in the body's world, to listen to the body, and to speak in its behalf, it is significant that the most common setting in which seminarians learn to engage in pastoral conversation is the hospital, the very place in our society where the body itself is the object of acute attention (and debasement). This connection between the hospital setting and the importance of learning to speak within and through the body's world has not, for the most part, been recognized, much less exploited, by those of us who teach seminarians how to engage in meaningful pastoral conversation. Yet it is interesting to note that Denise Levertov was herself a nurse during World War II, and is therefore exceptional among poets in her familiarity with the hospital. In "The Malice of Innocence"[42] she tells how the hospital world continues to exert a strong hold on her more than two decades later:

> A glimpsed world, halfway through the film,
> one slow shot of a ward at night
>
> holds me when the rest is quickly
> losing illusion. Strange hold,
>
> as of romance, of glamor: not because
> even when I lived in it I had
>
> illusions about that world: simply because
> I did live there and it was
>
> a world. Greenshaded lamp glowing
> on the charge desk, clipboards
> stacked on the desk for the night,
>
> sighs and waiting, waiting-for-morning stirrings
> in the dim long room, warm, orderly,
> and full of breathings as a cowbarn.
>
> Death and pain dominate this world, for though
> many are cured, they leave still weak,
>
> still tremulous, still knowing mortality
> has whispered to them; have seen in the folding
> of white bedspreads according to rule
>
> the starched pleats of a shroud.
> It's against that frozen
> counterpane, and the knowledge too
> how black an old mouth gaping at death can look

that the night routine has in itself—
without illusions—glamor, perhaps. It had

a rhythm, a choreographic decorum:
when all the evening chores had been done

and a multiple restless quiet listened
to the wall-clock's pulse, and turn by turn

the two of us made our rounds
on tiptoe, bed to bed,

counting by flashlight how many pairs
of open eyes were turned to us,

noting all we were trained to note,
we were gravely dancing—starched

in our caps, our trained replies,
our whispering aprons—the well-rehearsed

pavanne of power. Yes, wasn't it power,
and not compassion,

       gave our young hearts
their hard fervor? I hated

to scrub out lockers, to hand out trays of
unappetizing food, and by day, or the tail-end of night

(daybreak dull on gray faces—ours and theirs)
the anxious hurry, the scolding old-maid bosses.
But I loved the power
of our ordered nights,

    gleaming surfaces I'd helped to polish
making patterns in the shipshape
halfdark—
    loved
the knowing what to do, and doing it,
list of tasks getting shorter

hour by hour. And knowing
all the while that Emergency
might ring with a case to admit, anytime,

if a bed were empty. Poised,
ready for that.
            The camera
never returned to the hospital ward,

the story moved on into the streets,
into the rooms where people lived.

But I got lost in the death rooms a while,
remembering being (crudely, cruelly,
just as a soldier or one of the guards
from Dachau might be) in love with order,

an angel like the *chercheuses de poux,* floating
noiseless from bed to bed,

smoothing pillows, tipping
water to parched lips, writing

details of agony carefully into the Night Report.

The world of the hospital is one dominated by death, for even though
many are cured, they know as they leave the hospital that "mortality has
whispered to them" and that the white bedspreads could well have served as
shrouds. Her own perspective was, however, quite a different one, for what
she and the other young nurses felt in their hearts was not compassion for the
sick and dying but "the power of our ordered nights," as they went about
doing what they knew to do, poised to respond to any emergency that might
arise, and feeling the power that comes with establishing and keeping order.
How different was she, she asks, from the guards at Dachau who were also so
much in love with order?

This, of course, was a time in her life when, as we have already noted, her
poetry was itself abstract, unattentive to the experiences she herself was
having. Even as her poetry subsequently took on a very different tone, so she
is deeply critical of the attitude of this young, efficient nurse who had little
time for compassion for the sick and dying. "Death Psalm: O Lord of
Mysteries"[43] reflects this very different attitude toward death, especially death
that defies one's love for order, and instead insists on coming when it pleases:

She grew old.
She made ready to die.

She gave counsel to women and men, to young girls and
                                        young boys.
She remembered her griefs.
She remembered her happinesses.
She watered the garden.
She accused herself.
She forgave herself.
She learned new fragments of wisdom.
She forgot old fragments of wisdom.
She abandoned certain angers.
She gave away gold and precious stones.
She counted-over her handkerchiefs of fine lawn.
She continued to laugh on some days, to cry on others,
                                unfolding the design of her identity.
She practiced the songs she knew, her voice
                                        gone out of tune
                        but the breathing-pattern perfected.
She told her sons and daughters she was ready.
She maintained her readiness.
She grew very old.
She watched the generations increase.
She watched the passing of seasons and years.
She did not die.

She did not die but lies half-speechless, incontinent,
                        aching in body, wandering in mind
                        in a hosptial room.
A plastic tube, taped to her nose,
        disappears into one nostril.
Plastic tubes are attached to veins in her arms.
Her urine runs through a tube into a bottle under the bed.
On her back and ankles are black sores.

The black sores are parts of her that have died.
The beat of her heart is steady.
She is not whole.

She made ready to die, she prayed, she made her peace,
        she read daily from the lectionary.

She tended the green garden she had made,
    she fought off the destroying ants,
    she watered the plants daily
    and took note of their blossoming.
She gave sustenance to the needy.
She prepared her life for the hour of death.
But the hour has passed and she has not died.

O Lord of mysteries, how beautiful is sudden death
    when the spirit vanishes
    boldly and without casting
    a single shadowy feather of hesitation
    onto the felled body.

O Lord of mysteries, how baffling, how clueless
    is laggard death, disregarding
    all that is set before it
        in the dignity of welcome—
laggard death, that steals
        insignificant patches of flesh—
laggard death, that shuffles
past the open gate,
past the open hand,
past the open,
        ancient,
        courteously waiting life.

Note her physical descriptions of the woman, her incontinence, her bodily aches, her black sores. While the beat of her heart is steady, she is not whole. And why is death delayed? Why does death shuffle past the open gate and hand, past the open, ancient, courteously waiting life? The answer, if there is one, is hidden in the heart of the Lord of mysteries. Meanwhile, death continues to disregard the welcome that is set before it.

In this poem, Levertov has come a long way from the young nurse who floated "noiseless from bed to bed, smoothing pillows, tipping water to parched lips, writing details of agony carefully in the Night Report." The difference is in her abandonment of the world of disembodied language and her immersion in the world—and language—of the body. It is both terribly ironic and significant that it was not as a nurse, but as a poet, that she came to appreciate the significance of embodied language. In so doing, she relinquished the order of the Night Report for the Lord of mysteries, and began to write in a manner that calls to mind the biblical psalms, those ancient examples of embodied language.

Yet, if the ancient psalms speak of the body beset with pain, disease, and death, they also capture in words the body's capacity to sing from within. Listening to the language of the body requires that we attend not only to its sighs too deep for words but also to its affirmations of the goodness of life. In "A Man,"[44] Levertov writes about one who sings his life:

> "Living a life"—
> the beauty of deep lines
> dug in your cheeks.
>
> The years gather by sevens
> to fashion you. They are blind,
> but you are not blind.
>
> Their blows resound,
> they are deaf, those laboring
> daughters of the Fates,
>
> but you are not deaf,
> you pick out
> your own song from the uproar
>
> line by line,
> and at last throw back
> your head and sing it.

This, too, is the language of the body.

3. INVITING THE GRIEVING
BACK TO LIFE

I N *ALL OUR LOSSES, ALL OUR GRIEFS*, KENNETH R. MITCHELL AND HERBERT
Anderson write, "Experiences that evoke grief are both more frequent
and more varied than most people imagine. The death of a person one
loves is such an obvious occasion of grief that many people have come to
think of it as the only such occasion."[1] Grief, they point out, is an appropriate
response to any significant loss.

The six major types of loss, according to Mitchell and Anderson, are
material loss (loss of a physical object or of familiar surroundings to which one
has an important attachment); *relationship* loss (the ending of opportunities to
be in the emotional or physical presence, or both, of a particular other human
being); *intrapsychic* loss (the experience of losing an emotionally important
image of oneself); *functional* loss (loss of some of the muscular or neurological
functions of the body); *role* loss (the loss of a specific social role or one's
accustomed place in a social network); and *systemic* loss (the loss that a system
sustains when one part of the system leaves or functions very differently
within the system, as when a young adult departs from the family of origin).[2]

In addition to identifying losses according to type, Mitchell and Anderson
explore other variables inherent in the loss itself, focusing on these five:
avoidable and unavoidable loss; temporary and permanent loss; actual and
imagined loss; anticipated and unanticipated loss; and leaving and being left.[3]

A major theme throughout their book is the relationship between loss and
grieving over loss. In their discussion of grieving, they note that a common
reaction to loss is searching for the lost object. This is a normal and acceptable
form of grieving, for such searching for the lost object goes on in the present,
as though the lost object were still around just waiting to be seen or found, and
the grieving person is able to admit without difficulty that time has passed
since the loss occurred. An abnormal and unacceptable response to loss is

time-freezing, which is a denial of the passage of time, an attempt to stop time in its flight, as the grieving person attempts to dwell on, or in some cases actually to live in, the time just prior to the loss. Sometimes this takes the form of keeping a room or a portion of the house just as it was when the loved one was still present.[4]

Thus, where the search for the lost object involves an acceptance of the fact that the object is gone and will not return, time-freezing is an attempt to deny the loss, and to live as though no loss has actually occurred. The one is based on acceptance of loss, and is therefore a "faithful" response, while the other is based on a denial of loss, and is therefore an "unfaithful" response: "If, at a deep emotional level, the person who has suffered a loss denies the reality of that loss, the process of letting go is severely compromised."[5]

One of the goals of grieving, and one in which the pastor may provide assistance, is to gain emotional release from the attachment to the lost object, and this is done primarily by making the lost object a memory: "Reminiscing or remembering with another person is the principal means by which we build such a memory, which in turn helps us gain needed emotional distance from the past."[6]

Another "unfaithful" response to loss which Mitchell and Anderson do not discuss is the *rejection* of the lost object. This is a response that Sigmund Freud considers in his essay "Mourning and Melancholia."[7] Where mourning involves the relinquishing of the lost object, and thus an acceptance of the loss, melancholia is a turning against the lost object, by claiming (falsely) that we did not love it anyway, and, indeed, are better off without it. In addition to its being a relatively common response to relationship loss (e.g., due to death or divorce), this rejective response is common to social role loss, as when one retires from a job or occupation.

Thus, on one extreme, there is *denial* of the loss, and, on the other extreme, there is *rejection* of the lost object. Between these extremes, there is *acceptance* of the loss, and such acceptance is what true grieving achieves or realizes in time.

Acceptance, however, is a word that has a number of nuances of meaning, and, through the years, it has become increasingly evident to those involved in helping others grieve that some ways of talking about acceptance are genuinely consoling to those who have suffered a loss, while other ways of talking about acceptance only serve to make the other angry or upset. The difference seems to be that, in the former case, acceptance is talked about solely in terms of accepting the undeniable fact that a loss has occurred. When those advocating acceptance go further than this, and offer *reasons* for why the other should accept the loss, this is where problems occur, as the one who has sustained the loss often finds these reasons unconvincing or irrelevant. A useful distinction may therefore be made between acceptance as acceptance that a loss has been sustained (i.e., one neither denies that something has occurred nor that what has occurred is truly a loss), and acceptance of the loss for certain specified reasons.

Mitchell and Anderson touch on this issue in recounting a pastor's conversation with a woman who interprets her husband's stroke as a lesson from God:

Pastor: What are your feelings about the stroke now?

Beth: I think God was trying to teach us a lesson.

Pastor: A lesson?

Beth: I realize now we were not really focusing on God, but that we made money and financial security our God. We worked all those years to pay off the farm and put the kids through school, and we finally thought we were getting ahead when the stroke happened. Since the stroke, I've been thinking and I have come to the conclusion that God was trying to tell us we were to look to him for security and not to money. It's been hard, but I think we will be better off thinking about God more and money less.

The authors write, "Beth's way of making sense of her husband's stroke was to regard it as punishment from God. Rather than acknowledge that people have strokes because it is one kind of illness that people are capable of having, she interprets it as a harsh bit of divine pedagogy." They observe, however, that "this interpretation, though theologically deficient, was used by Beth to reorient her life and her faith. Her acceptance of the present for what it can be was informed by her gratitude that 'we still have time together.' "[8]

In effect, Beth has expressed two grounds for acceptance. One is that the loss had a reason behind it, this reason being that God was "trying to teach us a lesson." The other is that one accepts the fact of the loss and finds something positive, something to be grateful for, in the fact that "we still have time together." The second form of acceptance does not try to find a reason for the loss, but recognizes the fact of the loss while at the same time affirming that their life, while diminished, is still good, as they do have "time together." Ironically, what we may term the less "faithful" form of acceptance is the one attributed to God, while the more "faithful" form of acceptance is less overtly religious. As Mitchell and Anderson summarize the case, her acceptance of the fact of the loss and gratitude for remaining time together is not explicitly attributed to or associated with God.

William Stafford has written a number of poems concerning loss, and a common theme that runs through many of these is acceptance. What makes them especially valuable is that they address acceptance from the perspectives of both the one who has sustained a loss and the one who seeks to provide some solace, and they take the very position just set forth, that it is usually unhelpful to offer reasons why a loss should be accepted. His poems on loss are also valuable in actively making the lost object a memory, and thereby enabling the poet (and the reader) to gain needed emotional distance from the past.

To assist in organizing Stafford's poems on loss, I will use the categories that Mitchell and Anderson offer, beginning with poems on relationship loss, and, within this group, focusing first on poems that concern unavoidable loss and, secondly, on those that involve avoidable loss. All of these poems on relationship loss are written from the perspective of the one who has been left behind. Then I will consider poems that deal with functional and role loss, mainly due to aging. Some of the poems involving relationship loss have elements of intrapsychic loss as well, as the relationship loss in question—a daughter leaving home—has had an impact on the poet's image of himself as a loving father. Systemic loss is here implied as well.

RELATIONSHIP LOSS

In "Bess,"[9] Stafford recalls a woman who lived in his neighborhood and who died of cancer. Her courageous acceptance of her death was a gift she bestowed on those who were left behind, and Stafford is one who feels she should be remembered for this:

> Ours are the streets where Bess first met her
> cancer. She went to work every day past the
> secure houses. At her job in the library
> she arranged better and better flowers, and when
> students asked for books her hand went out
> to help. In the last year of her life
> she had to keep her friends from knowing
> how happy they were. She listened while they
> complained about food or work or the weather.

And the great national events danced
their grotesque, fake importance. Always

Pain moved where she moved. She walked
ahead; it came. She hid; it found her.
 No one ever served another so truly;
no enemy ever meant so strong a hate.
It was almost as if there was no room
left for her on earth. But she remembered
where joy used to live. She straightened its flowers;
she did not weep when she passed its houses;
and when finally she pulled into a tiny corner
and slipped from pain, her hand opened
again, and the streets opened, and she wished all well.

In "Madge,"[10] he depicts two persons (himself and, one guesses, his wife) who have returned home from attending a funeral. Here, the poem moves from talk about the circumstances of Madge's death and the possibility that more could have been done to keep her alive, to distracted thought about the funeral, and then to an expression of acceptance of the fact that a loss has been sustained:

Or you could do it, the speech I mean
at the end, after we come back and sit down
and look at each other. You could stare
into the fire, getting ready, then begin:
"Why did we pay any attention to her?
At the last you could see her—a shell created
by our habit of deferring, one long complaint
secretly wanting to be stopped. Brutality
could have saved her." You stir the fire.

Or I could do it, since no one else,
really, knew her that well. But my habit
of silence would stop me. Not yet could I
slouch down, put my feet up the way she never
liked, and begin to talk out the tangle
our lives had become. I would sweep the hearth:
"Did you see the flowers from the neighbors? All those

roses? And I liked what Josie said,
about the years." I'd stare at the fire.

Or, carefully, we both could say it: "She's gone."

The death of Stafford's father is the subject of the two following poems. In "Circle of Breath,"[11] which focuses on the night of his father's death, an experience they shared helps him to begin the process of lovingly but firmly relinquishing his father:

> The night my father died the moon shone on the snow.
> I drove in from the west; mother was at the door.
> All the light in the room extended like a shadow.
> Truant from knowing, I stood where the great dark fell.
>
> There was a time before, something we used to tell—
> how we parked the car in a storm and walked into a field
> to know how it was to be cut off, out in the dark alone.
> My father and I stood together while the storm went by.
>
> A windmill was there in the field giving its little cry
> while we stood calm in ourselves, knowing we could go home.
> But I stood on the skull of the world the night he died, and knew
> that I leased a place to live with my white breath.
>
> Truant no more, I stepped forward and learned his death.

In "Elegy,"[12] the grieving process continues, as Stafford mixes the remembering of shared experiences with a searching for his father, as though his father is still around and just waiting to be seen or heard:

> The responsible sound of the lawnmower
> puts a net under the afternoon;
> closing the refrigerator door
> I hear a voice in the other room
> that starts up color in every cell:
> > Presents like this, Father, I got from you,
> > and there are hundreds more to tell.
>
> One night, sound held in cornfield farms
> drowned in August, and melonflower breath

creeping in stealth—we walked west
where all the rest of the country slept.
I hold that memory in both my arms—
    how the families there had starved the dogs;
    in the night they waited to be fed.

At the edge of dark there paled a flash—
a train came on with its soft tread
that roused itself with light and thundered
with dragged windows curving down earth's side
while the cornstalks whispered.
    All of us hungry creatures watched
    until it was extinguished.

If only once in all those years
the right goodby could have been said!
I hear you climbing up the snow,
a brown-clad wanderer on the road
with the usual crooked stick,
    and on the wrong side of the mountains
    I can hear the latches click.

Remember in the Southwest going down the canyons?
We turned off the engine, the tires went hoarse
picking up sound out of turned away mountains;
we felt the secret sky lean down.
Suddenly the car came to with a roar.
    And remember the Christmas wreath on our door—
    when we threw it away and it jumped blue up the fire?

At sight of angels or anything unusual
you are to mark the spot with a cross,
for I have set out to follow you
and these marked places are expected,
but in between I can hear no sound.
    The softest hush of doors I close
    may jump to slam in a March wind.

When you left our house that night and went falling
into that ocean, a message came: silence.
I pictured you going, spangles and bubbles

leaving your pockets in a wheel clockwise.
Sometimes I look out of our door at night.
   When you send messages they come spinning
   back into sound with just leaves rustling.

Come battering. I listen, am the same, waiting.

Notice how much of this "elegy" for his father involves remembrances of experiences they shared. In "Father's Voice,"[13] he recalls sayings of his departed father, gifts that he continues to treasure:

"No need to get home early;
the car can see in the dark."
   He wanted me to be rich
   the only way we could,
   easy with what we had.

And always that was his gift,
given for me ever since,
   easy gift, a wind
   that keeps on blowing for flowers
   or birds wherever I look.

World, I am your slow guest,
one of the common things
   that move in the sun and have
   close, reliable friends
   in the earth, in the air, in the rock.

In "Stillborn,"[14] acceptance of the loss is reflected in his remembrance of the infant who almost lived:

Where a river touches an island
under willows leaning over
I watch the waves and think of you,
   who almost lived.

Stars will rake the sky again,
and time go on, the dark, the cold.
Clouds will race when the wind begins,
   where you almost were.

> But while the thunder shakes the world
> and the graceful dance and the powerful win,
> still faithful, still in thought, I bow,
>   little one.

In the preceding poems, memory is an essential means for Stafford to accept his loss, and the writing of a poem about the one he has lost is itself a means of recall. In none of these poems is there a denial of the loss or a rejection of the lost object. The search for the lost object is not in opposition to acceptance but is an expression of his acceptance of the loss. Reasons for the loss are not offered or even considered. The only thing that matters is the fact that a loss has been sustained, and this fact is fully accepted.

"In a Corner"[15] is about anticipatory loss and what it feels like to know that one is about to suffer loss:

> Walls hold each other up when they meet;
> a ceiling joins them: that corner you can
> study, in jail or hospital or school.
> I leaned in a corner once when someone
> was dying, and I didn't care if the rest
> of the walls went anywhere, or if the ceiling
> or floor, or if anything—I didn't care.
>
> Now if I'm traveling maybe a bad headache
> sends me to lean in a corner. Each eye
> has a wall. Father, Mother—they're gone,
> and that person died, when I leaned before.
> The corner never feels little enough,
> and I roll my head for the world, for its need
> and this wild, snuggling need and pain of my own.

This image of the corner captures our visceral response to death. Corners hold us in place, but do little else to comfort or console. They have associations with punishment, with being captured, with having nowhere to turn, no place to snuggle for warmth and solace.

The poems about Bess, his father, and the stillborn infant have in common the sense that the loss was unavoidable, that there was nothing that could have been done, humanly speaking, to avert the loss. "Madge," too, alludes to the fact that, had they not been so acquiescent (to the doctors' efforts to keep her alive?), Madge would have gone more quickly, as she wanted to go, and would not have died a mere "shell" of herself. There are several other poems, however, that focus on losses that were clearly avoidable, as they were not the result of circumstances or forces beyond human agency or control, but of human violence. In "Murder Bridge,"[16] Stafford recounts the story of the deaths of three children by their mother's own hand:

> You look over the edge, down, down . . . —
> there's where the poor crazy mother threw
> them, all three, her children she loved. They hurtled
> and struck far there, once, then whirled
> from rock to rock on into the rapid,
> were found miles on, pieces their mother
> had to see forever, the rest of her life.
>
> It's quiet here. The rocks dream in the sun.
> Our parents remembered the story. Our hands
> gripped white on the railing. We felt the earth tilt.
> We never thought the world was easy, as we
> drove on. Luck—it takes luck and the sun
> shining, and that mother recovered and crying
> in our world saying, "Little ones, little ones."

The Stafford children's reaction of horror in hearing the story of the terrible deaths of three other children is reflected in the hands gripping the rail and their sense that, this day, the earth itself had tilted. However, writing now, years later, he is also concerned for the mother, who lived the rest of her life with the memory of the children's broken bodies. Her "recovery" made her deed all the more difficult to live with, all the more unfathomable, as it was not that she did not love them.

A tragedy that was closer to home, as it involved a girl whom he had known, is recounted in "A Gesture Toward an Unfound Renaissance":[17]

> There was the slow girl in art class,
> less able to say where our lessons led: we
> learned so fast she could not follow us.
> But at the door each day I looked back
> at her rich distress, knowing almost enough
> to find a better art inside the lesson.

> And then, late at night, when the whole town
> was alone, the current below the rumbly bridge
> at Main Street would go an extra swirl
> and gurgle, once, by the pilings;
> and at my desk at home, or when our house
> opened above my bed toward the stars,
> I would hear that one intended lonely sound,
> the signature of the day, the ratchet of time
> taking me a step toward here, now, and this
> look back through the door that always closes.

Falling somewhere between avoidable and unavoidable losses are several poems about the apparent estrangement of his grown child from parents and home. Mitchell and Anderson would perhaps characterize these poems as dealing not only with relationship loss but also with intrapsychic and systemic loss. The first of these poems is titled "For a Child Gone to Live in a Commune":[18]

> Outside our ways you found
> a way, no name for your home,
> no number, not even words.
>
> I thought your voice held onto curves
> over cliffs when you said, "We let the animals
> have whatever they wanted."
>
> I forgot to tell you: this house too
> is a wanderer. Under its paint it is
> orbiting all I ever thought it would find—
>
> Those empty spaces. It has found them.

This poem seems to have a note of suppressed anger and defensiveness. The father who has championed freedom feels betrayed and resentful that a child of his believes there is greater freedom to be found in a commune. But in a later poem, "For a Lost Child,"[19] this note of anger and resentment is replaced by a nearly overwhelming longing for contact with his child who has wandered far:

> What happens is, the kind of snow that sweeps
> Wyoming comes down while I'm asleep. Dawn

finds our sleeping bag but you are gone.
Nowhere now, you call through every storm,
a voice that wanders without a home.

Across bridges that used to find a shore
you pass, and along shadows of trees that fell
before you were born. You are a memory
too strong to leave this world that slips away
even as its precious time goes on.

I glimpse you often, faithful to every country
we ever found, a bright shadow the sun
forgot one day. On a map of Spain
I find your note left from a trip that year
our family traveled: "Daddy, we could meet here."

Another poem, "Disposal,"[20] is also concerned with the estrangement of
father and daughter:

Paste her picture back of the mirror
and close it. Let landscape be
the focus of whatever the next scene is—
that's a face you can try to forget, and the weather
visits often this time of year.

You can throw her furniture out. Let the rain
decide what to keep and what to dissolve
or slash into bits, a ritual forgetting
that the world makes happen in its own way
from this time on, outside or in.

Now slowly release her name. It spins
miles long like a thread along the wind.

This poem has an aggressive tone similar to "For a Child Gone to Live in a
Commune": "you can throw her furniture out" and the rain will "slash" some
of it "into bits." Yet, it ends with a more gentle image of weaving, as her
name, released, "spins miles long like a thread along the wind." However
successful one may be in "releasing" the other, enlisting the world in this
"ritual forgetting," the thread is miles long and carried by the wind. This
poem, then, takes note of the difficulty involved in accepting loss, loss which

in this case is relational, systemic, and intrapsychic, all in one. Yet the poem itself—the very act of writing it—is a searching for the lost object. He need only "release her name" and it goes spinning out, carried by the wind.

FUNCTIONAL LOSS

A number of Stafford's more recent poems focus on functional loss due to aging and its debilitating effects. In "Waiting in Line,"[21] a poem that offers a litany of the losses to which the "very old" are subject also strikes a strong note of acceptance:

> You the very old, I have come
> to the edge of your country and looked across,
> how your eyes warily look into mine
> when we pass, how you hesitate when
> we approach a door. Sometimes
> I understand how steep your hills
> are, and your way of seeing the madness
> around you, the careless waste of the calendar,
> the rush of people on buses. I have
> studied how you carry packages,
> balancing them better, giving them attention.
> I have glimpsed from within the gray-eyed look
> at those who push, and occasionally even I
> can achieve your beautiful bleak perspective
> on the loud, the inattentive, shoving boors
> jostling past you toward their doom.
>
> With you, from the pavement I have watched
> the nation of the young, like jungle birds
> that scream as they pass, or gyrate on playgrounds,
> their frenzied bodies jittering with the disease
> of youth. Knowledge can cure them. But
> not all at once. It will take time.
>
> There have been evenings when the light
> has turned everything silver, and like you
> I have stopped at a corner and suddenly
> staggered with the grace of it all: to have
> inherited all this, or even the bereavement

of it and finally being cheated!—the chance
to stand on a corner and tell it goodby!
Every day, every evening, every
abject step or stumble has become heroic:—

You others, we the very old have a country.
A passport costs everything there is.

In "Not Having Wings,"[22] he continues his exploration into the older person's country, celebrating his own attitude of being at peace with himself and the world, and of being content, in lieu of miracles, with the gracefulness of everyday life:

If I had a wing it might hurt,
be broken. I would trail it
around, stumbling on it. Maybe infection
sets in. Tortured by terrible pain,
I forget all about God and curse
and am lost. I'm glad I don't have any wings.

Now when I hobble, it is an act
of mercy for that knee, the one
relied on so often in the sugar-beet fields.
I get somewhere; I relax, letting
me and the rest of the world balance
again: Take it easy, World, old friend.

Here, as in "Waiting in Line," he uses the image of "balancing" to understand the aging person's experiences in the world. Even as one learns to balance packages, and to maintain one's balance while walking, one also learns to strike a proper balance between oneself and the rest of the world, even to the point of admonishing the world, one's lifelong friend, to take it easy too. As with his previous poems on functional loss, this one, too, has a strong note of acceptance.

In "Revelation,"[23] Stafford recounts his own near-experience of death—being thrown off his bike onto the pavement—and his subsequent anticipation of the actual event of death:

When I came back to earth, it was my bike
threw me. I woke to day not real day—

87

some of the sunlight came like bottles piled
in a window frame. People were pictured with labels,
"Doctor," "intern," "aide." I remember a cookie
big as the sun that lasted as long as a glass of milk.

Some day your world won't last all day. You'll blink;
you'll fall to earth; and where the ocean was
will be that color *here* was before you came:
your head and what you hit will sound the same.

In "Rescue,"[24] which apparently alludes to the same encounter with death, Stafford shifts from the lesson it taught him about his eventual death to what he learned from this experience for living, namely, that reaching out to the dead gives inspiration for going on with one's life:

A fire was burning. In another room
somebody was talking. Sunlight slanted
across the foot of my bed, and a glass of water
gleamed where it waited on a chair near my hand.
I was alive and the pain in my head
was gone. Carefully I tried thinking
of those I had known. I let them walk
and then run, and then open their mouths the way
it used to cause the throbbing. It didn't hurt
anymore. Clearer and clearer I stared
far into the glass. I was cured.

From now on in my life there would be a place
like a scene in a paperweight. One figure in the storm
would be reaching out with my hand for those
who had died. It would always be still in that scene,
no matter what happened. I could come back to it,
carefully, any time, to be saved, and go on.

In "Yellow Flowers,"[25] about the same encounter with death, he sees and recalls sights, and hears sounds, that bring him back to life:

While I was dying I saw a flower
by the road—yellow, with a rough
green stem. It had what I always

admire—patience, and the one great
virtue, being only itself. I was lying
where the wreck had thrown me, and I heard my pulse
telling me, "Come back, come back, come back."

I remembered a candle. It was at the end
of a row in church. Wind made it flicker.
It almost went out, but came back when left
alone. World with your flower, your candle:—
we flicker and bend; we hear wheels
on the road—any sight, any sound—that music
the soul takes and makes it its own.

In each of these poems about his encounter with death, Stafford is aware
that he came very close to losing everything, that he was suspended between
the world he had known and the world of the dead. In that moment, he found
himself reaching out to those who had gone before, and, at the same time, he
was able to remember scenes in his earlier life, especially the scene of a candle
in church whose light would flicker dangerously and then come back when
left alone. As in the poems about others who had actually died, there is no
attempt in these poems to give reasons for why this terrible accident had
happened to him. Instead, there is an acceptance of the fact that he very
nearly died, and gratitude for the fact that his life was spared.

Stafford is concerned in "The Book About You"[26] with what it is like to
discover that you are afflicted with a serious disease and have no idea how
long you might be able to stay alive:

The book that tells about you slumps in the library
somewhere in the medical section. It is vague at first
but then detailed: you are hopeless and not even interesting.
Cases like yours routine through hospitals, especially
in slum districts. By the end of the book, you are dead
one-third of the time but live a useful life
occasionally if treated early. One patient
in Calcutta lived fifteen years. Softly you close
the book and push back. You walk past the travel section
and the mysteries and romances. At the door you turn for a glance:
they have established a new shelf—pay books. The librarian
is watching you. You spread your hands, go out

the quiet door, and stand there enjoying the sun.
There are days like this for everyone. Somebody else
will put the book back. Strangely—one of the symptoms?—
you feel like singing.

In this, as in so many of Stafford's poems, there is neither denial of loss nor rejection of what is being lost, but an attitude of acceptance, an acceptance that needs no reason or rationale.

Being informed that one has a potentially terminal illness is a very serious matter. Far less serious is the occasion of one's birthday. And yet, in "The Only Card I Got on My Birthday Was from an Insurance Man,"[27] Stafford addresses the fact that a birthday may evoke anticipations of one's eventual death:

On upland farms into abandoned wells
on a line meridian high
state by state my birthday star comes on
and peers, my birthday night,
and in my eyes it stands while past its light
the world and I turn, just and far, till
every well scans over the year like spokes
of a wheel returning the long soft look of the sky.

Star in a well, dark message: when I die,
my glance drawn over galaxies,
all through one night let a candle nurse the dark
to mark this instant of what I was,
this once—not putting my hand out
blessing for business' sake any frail markers
of human years: we want real friends or none;
what's genuine will accompany every man.

Who travel these lonely wells can drink that star.

Birthdays are, of course, a time for the lighting of candles. He asks only that there also be a candle lit for a single night to mark his passing. Thus, as in "Yellow Flowers," the candle symbolizes our lives: how we flicker and bend and then, in time, go out. In another poem about functional loss, entitled "Strokes,"[28] he suggests that upbeat words from a minister, while not altogether truthful, are like lighted candles for the old:

The left side of her world is gone—
the rest sustained by memory
and a realization: There are still the children.

Going down our porch steps her pastor
calls back: "We are proud of her recovery,
and there is a chiropractor up in Galesburg. . . ."

The birthdays of the old require such candles.

EXTENDING AN INVITATION

In most of the poems we have reviewed thus far, Stafford speaks from the perspective of the one who has sustained a loss, and who is faced with the task of accepting it. In several other poems, however, he looks at loss and grieving from a different perspective, focusing on the efforts of those who seek to provide consolation to others. In a poem entitled, appropriately, "Consolations,"[29] he identifies some of the clichés that the grieving often hear from others, and indicates why these are doomed to fail:

"The broken part heals even stronger than the rest,"
they say. But that takes awhile.
And, "Hurry up," the whole world says.
They tap their feet. And it still hurts on rainy
afternoons when the same absent sun
gives no sign it will ever come back.

"What difference in a hundred years?"
The barn where Agnes hanged her child
will fall by then, and the scrawled words
erase themselves on the floor where rats' feet
run. Boards curl up. While new trees
drink what the rivers bring. Things die.

"No good thing is easy." They told us that,
while we dug our fingers into the stones
and looked beseechingly into their eyes.
They say the hurt is good for you. It makes
what comes later a gift all the more
precious in your bleeding hands.

These cliché consolations ignore the fact that it still hurts long after it was supposedly better than new, that terrible suffering has occurred, and that the bleeding doesn't stop just because consoling words have been spoken. In fact, each of these so-called consolations is terribly insensitive to the pain and suffering the other now endures and may well endure throughout the remaining years of life. These are very different from the words of the pastor in "Strokes," who knows full well that he is talking a kind of nonsense, and that the others know it too. Rather, these "consolations" are offered in all seriousness, with an air of authoritativeness, when, in fact, the speaker is stupid, insensitive, or both.

In place of such cliché consolations, Stafford offers, in "Confessor,"[30] the simple prescription of listening, remembering what we have heard, and keeping it to ourselves:

> The girl hiding in the hall on the ferry
> from Alaska, the old man who kept his face
> in shadow, that matron shuddering over
> the market basket in the parking lot—
> scores of these follow me into my dreams,
> and I can't tell more because I promised.
>
> I carry their burden. When I go down
> the street my memory is a vault that no one
> need see opened. I am their plain
> unmarked envelope that passes through the world.
> People tell me what they don't want to carry
> alone. They have felt singled out by some
> blow: not always at fault but still
> ashamed for a human involvement, they want
> someone else to know, to bear with them
> and not blame. I am their stranger and will pass
> out of their life. . . .
>
> All right. I listen. My life sinks a little
> farther, for the pity; from now on I know it
> with them. We'll take a stand, wherever the end is.
> We go forward by this quiet sharing,
> they one way, I another. I am their promise:
> no one else is going to know.

These sufferers know that their stories will not go any further, that he will not compound their burden by revealing to others what has been disclosed to him. Nor will he blame. The "quiet sharing" seems to help as each is able to go forward. The other's need to tell her story has not gone unmet. This much the confessor has been able to give.

There are other poems by Stafford that suggest there are times when those who are suffering simply cannot be consoled. The woman who murdered her three children is one example. In the following poem, entitled "Scars,"[31] he observes a woman whose sorrows cannot even be reached through music:

> They tell how it was, and how time
> came along, and how it happened
> again and again. They tell
> the slant life takes when it turns
> and slashes your face as a friend.
>
> Any wound is real. In church
> a woman lets the sun find
> her cheek, and we see the lesson:
> there are years in that book; there are sorrows
> a choir can't reach when they sing.
>
> Rows of children lift their faces of promise,
> places where the scars will be.

Yet, if some of his poems imply that there are losses so great and so deep, or so many over the course of a lifetime, that they are beyond the capacity of others to assuage, there are other poems that, without giving reasons for why we should accept a loss, extend the invitation to do so. In "It's All Right,"[32] he gives no reasons why a person should accept the loss, but he offers the observation that never is the whole world totally against us, that always some segment of the world cares, and this in itself is consoling:

> Someone you trusted has treated you bad.
> Someone has used you to vent their ill temper.
> Did you expect anything different?
> Your work—better than some others—has languished,
> neglected. Or a job you tried was too hard,
> and you failed. Maybe weather or bad luck

spoiled what you did. That grudge, held against you
for years after you patched up, has flared,
and you've lost a friend for a time. Things
at home aren't so good; on the job your spirits
have sunk. But just when the worst bears down
you find a pretty bubble in your soup at noon,
and outside at work a bird says, "Hi!"
Slowly the sun creeps along the floor;
it is coming your way. It touches your shoe.

How is this poem any different from the cliché consolations that Stafford
disparages in "Consolations"? If he had said, "It's always darkest before the
dawn," he would have denied the loss with cliché wisdom that claims to be
based on some universal law. Instead, he offers, for what it is worth, an
observation about how, just when the worst bears down, and we feel we just
can't take it anymore, something small and seemingly insignificant occurs that
lifts our spirits sufficiently to carry on. This poem, then, extends an invitation to
notice those small, seemingly insignificant—even trivial— occurrences that say
to us that the world is not all bad. It is the very insignificance of the bubble in
the soup, the bird's cheery "hi," and the sun touching one's shoe that lifts our
spirits and quickens our resolve to go on with living.

Had he offered strong and persuasive reasons for why we must accept our
loss and get on with life—"You owe it to your children" or "You have too
much to offer"—we who are grieving may appropriately dismiss these as
well-intentioned but clumsy attempts to persuade us that our loss is not as bad
as we think it is. Acceptance of our loss is not based on any reasons or
arguments of this kind, but is a response to a world that is capable, in its own,
unpredictable ways, of lifting our spirits just enough to enable us to accept the
invitation to go on living.

Mitchell and Anderson define grieving as "a process in which our attachments to the lost person or object are not entirely given up, but are sufficiently
altered to permit the grieving person to admit the reality of the loss and then to
live without constant reference to it."[33] They add, "In successful grieving, the
mourner gradually becomes able to make attachments and investments in other
persons and things once again."[34] What Stafford contributes to the grieving
process is the observation—to say the "conviction" would be too strong and
definite—that the world, for all its capacity to inflict pain and hurt, is a pretty
good place to be. If the desired outcome of the grieving process is a reinvestment
in life, then he is saying, through his poetic gifts, that the decision to reinvest is

appropriate and valid, for the world is a good place, and, on balance, life in this world is a precious thing. If this were not so, we would not feel so terribly sorry for the ones we have lost, in spite of the fact that they suffered so.

THE BOY WHO TASTED HEAVEN ON EARTH

It was not through philosophical or theological reflection that Stafford came by his sense that the world is a pretty good place to be. It was more direct than this. In an autobiographical essay, he relates the following experience: "I was in Liberal [Kansas] High School, and one autumn afternoon on a weekend I got on my bike . . . and rode ten or twelve miles to the Cimarron River northeast of town."[35] He climbed the riverbank, and from that vantage observed the open land, the setting sun, the emerging stars, and the rising sun the next morning: "That encounter with the size and serenity of the earth and its neighbors in the sky has never left me. The earth was my home. I could never feel lost while it held me."[36]

In "A Day to Remember,"[37] he describes a scene similar to the one recounted in his autobiographical essay:

> I'm standing at Lakeside Drive with my bike.
> It is dusk. I didn't think anybody would care
> if I'm lonely, a bicycle in traffic, young
> and hence guilty, some kind of oddity nobody
> would have. And here came this wind. Sometimes
> even snow is *for* you somehow, and this was.
> I belonged. It was 1935, the day
> I became saved and a citizen of the world.

Note his use of religious language to characterize his emotional state prior to the coming of the wind—"guilty"—and to capture how he felt afterward— "saved." Even as new converts typically feel a new sense of belonging, this happened for him as well: the world, through the gracious wind, had received him, addressed his loneliness, and made him its citizen. Also, as with religious conversions, this one came unbidden, unanticipated, and unplanned, supporting his view—expressed in the poem, "The Gospel Is Whatever Happens"[38]—that saving events occur through yielding:

> When we say, "Breath,"
> a feather starts to fly,

95

> to be itself.
> When we talk, truth
> is what we mean to say.
>
> A weather vane is
> courteous and accurate:
> the more it yields,
> the more wind lies
> where it points the way.

In "Waiting for God,"[39] he suggests that the simple act of breathing—in and out—is our way of participating, in a quiet, yielding way, in the rhythms of the earth:

> This morning I breathed in. It had rained
> early and the sycamore leaves tapped
> a few drops that remained, while waving
> the air's memory back and forth
> over the lawn and into our open
> window. Then I breathed out.
>
> This deliberate day eased
> past the calendar and waited. Patiently
> the sun instructed shadows how to move;
> it held them, guided their gradual defining.
> In the great quiet I carried my life on,
> in again, out again.

Another poem, "Local Events,"[40] tells how the earth, in its quiet, imperceptible way, was also there for him when he felt his very life was about to come to a violent end:

> A mouth said a bad word. A foot
> kicked me. One brick in the pavement
> stared into my left eye, and a noise
> came close and closer—a siren.
>
> "Listen," someone said, "he asked
> for it." Feet shuffled and the sun

went out in a fading glow. A red color
spread slowly across the road.

Then there wasn't any world. No one
was left anywhere, and in the quiet
a long breath shuddered gently out of
something in the road that used to be alive.

Air like the breath from our cellar lifted me
far where the sun was still shining.

As these several poems and his autobiographical recollections indicate, it
is the *natural* world to which Stafford turns, time and again, to support his
apprehension of the world, and of life, as inherently good. Yet two poems that
recount incidents when he was a boy suggest that the *human* world is also the
basis for belief in the goodness of life. The first such incident is recounted in
"Adults Only":[41]

Animals own a fur world;
people own worlds that are variously, pleasingly, bare.
And the way these worlds *are* once arrived for us kids with a jolt,
that night when the wild woman danced
in the giant cage we found we were all in
at the state fair.

Better women exist, no doubt, than that one,
and occasions more edifying, too, I suppose.
But we have to witness for ourselves what comes for us,
nor be distracted by barkers of irrelevant ware;
and a pretty good world, I say, arrived that night
when that woman came farming right out of her clothes,
by God,

At the state fair.

Here, too, the language of religion—"edifying," "witness," "by God"—is
used to capture a very this-worldly epiphany. Beneath these words is the
sense, also derived from religion, of surrendering oneself, opening oneself to
the workings of the spirit. There is nothing premeditated or self-conscious in
this, no adolescent bravado or defiant determination to do something wild or

forbidden. Instead, the wildness was in the spectacle, and "us kids" were the innocent recipients of a gift that was totally unexpected and ever so graceful: "A pretty good world, I say, arrived that night" when she came "farming"— note the pastoral image—"right out of her clothes."

The second episode was much like the first, as it also involved a beatific vision of sorts, this time involving the lion tamer's associate. The poem is entitled "Barnum and Bailey":[42]

> And also besides, listen, in addition, there was
> parked beyond the elephants a wagon with pictures on both
> sides where she lived, the woman with the legs, captive
> to the lion tamer, that cruel man with a chair
> and a mustache.
>
> The woman with the legs was washing her hair in sunshine
> when we peeked through a hole in the canvas around
> their wagon. The mustache man lazily was flipping
> a whip at a painted barrel in the golden light.
>
> Listen—you never know in your life when Heaven
> will come. It has to be chance. And you never get back.

Now the sighting of the woman is represented as the sudden, unexpected arrival of Heaven on earth. We could perhaps ask why these experiences of the world as a "pretty good" place involved women, and worldly women at that, but to engage in a deep psychoanalysis of the poet on the basis of these two poems would be to get caught up in the very distractions that he warns about in "Adults Only." The point is that there is a world out there that offers its odd moments of grace, many of which are even more glorious in our memory's eye.

It may seem strange to conclude a chapter on the acceptance of loss with poems about a boy's experience of viewing women at the state fair. But our question was, what is behind Stafford's invitation to those who have suffered grievous losses to accept their loss and go on living in spite of them? The answer lies in his experience, and his belief that his experience is not unique, of the world's ability to reach out and embrace us in unanticipated and unexpectedly gracious ways. Denial of our losses is futile. Rejection of that which we have loved and lost is dishonest, neither true to the other nor true to ourselves. The only way is the way of acceptance, which is assisted by memory, but also by yielding to the world's caring and loving embrace.

My purpose in this chapter has not been to provide a complete model for pastoral care of the grieving. This is already available in *All Our Losses, All Our Griefs*, where Mitchell and Anderson devote many pages to the pastoral response to those who grieve, providing full chapters each on personal and public ministries to the grieving, and on the theology of grieving. My goals are much more modest: to underscore the fact that acceptance of loss does not require reasons, for acceptance is reason enough.

Ever since I wrote about the biblical psalms of lament and suggested psalms for specific types of loss which pastors might read to grieving parishioners,[43] I have myself turned time and again both to psalms and to contemporary poetry—often simultaneously—as a personal resource in my own struggles with personal loss. Poetry is a wonderful resource—music being another—of coming to terms with our loss, as it encourages us to continue holding our loved ones in our hearts while releasing them from our grasp. I have taken Stafford's "Elegy," the poem about his father's death, as my own "psalm" of lament.

To what Mitchell and Anderson have to say about pastoral response to those who grieve, I add only this: Besides listening to the other's story of pain and remorse, the pastor's role is to invite the other—when ready—to accept the hospitality the world offers to all of its guests, most of the time. It was Job's counselor friends who tried to give reasons for all of Job's losses; it was God who did not give reasons but extended Job an invitation to take renewed interest in the world around him.[44]

4. LEARNING TO HEED
THE UNHEARD VOICES

I N *THE ABUSE OF POWER: A THEOLOGICAL PROBLEM,* JAMES POLING OFFERS this definition of practical theology: "Practical theology is theological interpretation of the unheard voices of personal and community life for the purpose of continual transformation of faith in the true God of love and power toward renewed ministry practice."[1] In explaining why "the unheard voices of personal and community life" are so important to practical theology, Poling notes, "Reflection begins with the presence of difference and otherness in experience. Difference provokes thought. When persons or communities become aware of some desire that contrasts with identity, the potential contradiction requires reflection. . . . Without difference and contrast, there can be no self-conscious experience."[2]

Poling's own study, based on the experiences of victims of sexual abuse and the perpetrators of such abuse, is an excellent example of how unheard voices, once heard, confront us with otherness in experience, and how the presence of such difference provokes thought. In contexts where the victims of sexual abuse have not had a voice, their stories, when heard, have a dramatic effect, as they present hearers with a potential contradiction between their previous thinking or assumptions about matters of victimization and abuse and what they are now being asked to consider. Poling's juxtaposition of the personal stories of the victims of sexual abuse with the personal stories of child molesters evokes a particularly powerful contradiction, for this juxtaposition dramatically heightens the reader's sense of the presence of difference and otherness in experience. For Poling himself, it was the personal stories of child molesters, told to him in the context of therapy, that provoked the greatest amount of dissonance within himself, as he has had to struggle with the question of why he has been both willing to work with individuals who are guilty of such acts and extremely uncomfortable in their presence:

One reason I am so uncomfortable with molesters is that I fear the fragmentation they exhibit and I wish to reject them as if they were the cause of my fragmentation. This is related to my real struggle to face my own fragility. Rejecting them is easier than admitting to myself that I am unintegrated and that my psychic self is only minimally held together by an intellectualized ego and a rigid superego. How much do I really know about my own symbiotic dependency and destructive aggression? I have found out that my professional identity often serves a defensive function in keeping my ugly parts hidden and sustaining the myth that I am a caring, humble person and interested only in helping those less fortunate.[3]

Thus, as he points out in explaining his definition of practical theology, "Reflection leads to awareness of tensions within the self. Perception of otherness and difference in experience enables one to see that the self is a fragile construction that needs continual transformation. Previous assumptions about this balance are challenged, and hidden desires of the heart are made manifest."[4]

A very interesting illustration of the fact that pastors have often been oblivious to voices unlike their own is presented in Jeanne Stevenson Moessner and Maxine Glaz's introduction to their coedited book, *Women in Travail and Transition:*

June, a mother for the first time, had had a harrowing delivery: she nearly died in childbirth. Exhausted and frightened, she lay awake in her hospital bed unable to close her eyes. She was glad that the birthing process was finished, but the baby, she felt, had nearly killed her. When her pastor arrived, five hours had passed since the ordeal.

She could not bring herself to describe her feelings: the pastor, aware that she had been near death, did not enquire. Instead, after introductory talk, the pastor repeated how grateful to God she should be for the wonderful new life that had been entrusted to her. June felt even worse after the visit because one major part of her experience had not been acknowledged: the baby as threat to her own life.[5]

If the story ended there, one would conclude that there was nothing more here than a missed opportunity to provide effective pastoral care. But there is more:

June did not establish a nonambivalent relationship with her infant. In therapy years later, she concluded that the emotions formed at the birth and sealed inside by the pastor's oblivious remarks were a significant factor in her lack of bonding with her child. Because she could not bring herself to share her feelings, she felt victimized, increasingly guilty, and cornered as the mother of this child. The outcome of this, she surmised, was a troubled adolescent.[6]

Moessner and Glaz ask: "Can a thirty-minute pastoral visit have such reverberations for a mother when the unspoken cry of her plight is missed or ignored? June thought so."[7] What the pastor failed to recognize or acknowledge in this episode was the factor of difference. From his point of view, every birth is occasion for expressing gratitude to God. But this woman's experience of birth was not a moment for gratitude and rejoicing. The pastor was oblivious to this very obvious difference. She was aware of it, but helpless at the time to protest or give voice to the anger that came out years later in the course of therapy. Until then, her own voice went undetected and unheard.

Emma Justes relates an even more blatant example of a pastoral counselor who refused to hear the victim's own voice, choosing instead to put the whole matter in his own words and his own terms.[8]

> Dorothy was a timid 23-year-old who had recently left her husband Joe after only a year of marriage. Her history included a life of domination by her mother who still called her every day, and inability to take over management of her own life. She had taken the step to leave Joe and was struggling with a decision about divorce or returning to work out a better relationship with him. . . . She visited a pastoral counselor not certain about what she wanted from counseling but needing help in finding direction in her life.

After she described her present situation, the pastoral counselor asked how she felt about her situation:

Dorothy: I'm—I guess—I'm feeling very bad.
Counselor: You're feeling very badly about it.
Dorothy: And I don't want it to be a—don't want to be a failure at the marriage and—I don't—and—I'd rather us be, you know, together. I don't—I just can't live with him.

Counselor: You left him, that's what I understand. Well, you feel bad, uh—uh—and did I catch you saying that you felt you had failed, or you don't want to feel that you've failed?

Dorothy: Well, I guess both things. And I feel as though I have—I—I mean I always thought that—I—when I got married it was going to be forever and (*pause*) . . .

Counselor: Yes?

Dorothy: . . . that's the way it was supposed to be and that's the way it would be for me.

Counselor: How do you feel towards him now?

Dorothy: (*pause*) Well, I guess—I just—you know really—still love him but I can't live with him.

Counselor: Would you care to tell me why?

Dorothy: Ah—because he doesn't care about me.

Counselor: Ummm, you don't feel that he loves you?

Dorothy: No. I don't think he ever did.

Counselor: Well, then you pulled out of the relationship to protect something. What was it you wanted to protect?

Dorothy: (pause) I guess—ah—it got so I didn't know what—what— anything was true—what—was true about anything but it was. I would think things were one way and he would say, "No they are another way," and so I didn't even know what I was feeling about anything.

Counselor: Well, how were you reacting to his attitudes toward you as a person?

Dorothy: Well, I guess I would cry a lot and then sometimes I'd get angry. It was very—it made me very—you know—very unhappy. It made me feel bad about myself.

Counselor: Were you able to sit down and talk to him about what he was doing to you?

Dorothy: I tried to and then he would say, "No, that's not right."

Counselor: In other words, your judgments about his attitude toward you were not right. Which would mean then, I would suppose, that he would recognize he really loves you. You were feeling neglected by him but he's saying, "No, you're wrong." So what does that mean? What is he saying?

Dorothy: Well, that sounds as though he does.

Counselor: It would *seem* so. Now, did you ever ask him what his reactions are to your attitudes? You've told him what your attitudes are and what your attitudes are to his reactions. Have you ever asked him how he's reacting to you?

Dorothy: Yes. But he won't say anything about it.

When the pastoral counselor was asked about his interpretation of Dorothy's situation he responded:

Well, I think—I think she acted just in the typically *inarticulate* and *dumb* way that many wives do who are—ah—who are lousing up their marriage. I think that if the facts were known—ah—the young man is filled with all kinds of resentment because—ah—things are not in good order when he comes home and—ah—expresses his resentment by throwing his stuff around and he can't—ah—feel gracious and cordial in relation to his wife so he doesn't say anything. And the possibilities are that if she could—ah—shape up and really fulfill his expectancies which don't sound like—ah—too great—and it would really sweeten him up and their marriage could get going again.

He went on to add that he saw Dorothy as a "slob" and a type that he had "run into before."

Justes writes, "The attitude of this counselor toward Dorothy expressed blame and contempt toward her. He saw her as the one who was to blame for the difficulties in the marriage relationship. It was a matter of her more effectively performing roles expected of one who is female. If she filled her role better Joe would be more amenable and the marriage would work."[9]

We might add that the counselor treated her much as she said Joe had been treating her. He challenged the truth of virtually everything she said to him, and totally ignored her observation that Joe probably never did love her. The whole premise on which he operates is that her perceptions and judgments are inaccurate, and that his own, though based on very little knowledge of the actual situation, are reliable and trustworthy. After all, he has "run into" this type of woman before. For this counselor, in spite of the fact that he has spent an hour with her discussing some very intimate matters, Dorothy remains an "unheard voice." Very little of what she said got through to him.

What these case illustrations provided by Poling, Moessner and Glaz, and Justes reveal is that when one offers pastoral care to persons or groups of persons who are different from oneself, one's own assumptions and values are called into question. Typically, in such situations, it is the one who offers pastoral care for whom this encounter is, potentially, the most life-changing. Those whom we intend to help may in fact be helped, and we may take appropriate credit for having helped them, yet it is often the case that the pastoral care person is the one who experiences greater personal or self-change, precisely because it is we who have encountered difference.

Denise Levertov's poetry has been helpful to me personally in precisely the same way. When I read the work of William Stafford, I feel that I am on rather familiar ground, as he is a man, he is from the Midwest and the Pacific Northwest, he went to public schools, he has been married to the same woman for many years, and he has had little interest in political action. In contrast, Denise Levertov is a woman, born and reared in England, who received no formal education but grew up in a home swirling with cultural and political activity. She had illustrious Jewish ancestors, immigrated to the United States as an adult and settled in New York City, and was actively involved in the antiwar movement of the 1960s.

For me to read the poetry of Denise Levertov is to be confronted with the difference of which Poling speaks. Hers is a voice—or, better, a chorus of voices—that for many years of my life I simply did not hear. When I did begin to listen to voices such as hers, it was apparent to me—and obvious to those whose voices they were—that I and not they was the one for whom this encounter was most life-changing. This was true even though I was assuming the role of teacher, pastor, or counselor, and they were student, parishioner, or counselee. I don't think that I was ever quite as insensitive or unhearing as the counselor in the case of Dorothy, but I am certain that I have been as oblivious to women's experience as the pastor in the case of June.

I view this chapter, then, as providing the occasion or setting for Denise Levertov to speak as a woman, a mother, a sister, and a daughter. In a sense, this chapter is intended for other men, like me, for whom the woman's voice is still somewhat alien and foreign—even though it has surrounded us since birth—and for whom the things that matter to women are threatening, puzzling, or all too easily ignored. There are many women poets whom I could have chosen for this purpose—Anne Sexton, Sylvia Plath, Adrienne Rich, Elizabeth Bishop, Sharon Olds, to name just a few—but Denise Levertov's poetry is uniquely invitational: It welcomes the male reader into the world of women's experience and makes every effort to put him at ease. This is not to say that there is no anger or rage in Levertov's world, nor is it to suggest that Levertov does not have some hard truths to say about men. But it *is* to say that because Levertov knows who *she* is and is at peace with her true self, men do not pose a personal threat for her. This sense of knowing who she is is beautifully expressed in her poem "Movement":[10]

> Towards not being
> anyone else's center
> of gravity.
>   A wanting
> to love: not
> to lean over towards
> an other, and fall,
> but feel within one
> a flexible steel
> upright, parallel
> to the spine but
> longer, from which to stretch;
> one's own
> grave springboard; the outflying spirit's
> vertical trampoline.

The making of a woman who is not "anyone else's center of gravity" begins in childhood, especially in the hard trials to which membership in a family exposes her. In Levertov's case, the family was a powerful crucible because it was virtually the totality of her experience as a child. By focusing on her poems about her family, we gain vivid impressions of her childhood, the world in which her sense of womanhood took root.

THE FAMILY CRUCIBLE

Levertov's poem "A New Year's Garland for My Students/MIT: 1969–70"[11] consists of thirteen vignettes of the members of a poetry seminar. Of "Judy" she writes:

> You have the light step
> of Ariel, the smile of Puck,
> something of Rosalind's
> courage, I think, though you are small
> as I imagine Perdita to have been

(and why Shakespeare gets into all this at all
I don't know—but he does, insistently)

but when you set off alone, winter nights,
coat collar up, and in your pocket
that invisible flute,

it's myself I think of, 12 years old,
trudging home from the library lugging
too many books, and seeing

visions in Ilford High Road,

the passing faces oblivious
to all their own strange beauty under the street-lamps,

and I drunk on it.

She identifies with Judy, who reminds her of herself at twelve years old, a small girl of light step, a ready smile, and a great deal of courage. In the Levertov household, all three were necessary if one wanted, as she surely did, to have and to be her own center of gravity and not become a self imposed by others.

In an autobiographical sketch written in 1984, she relates that "the Levertovs lived in Ilford because my father had been given (in the mistaken supposition that he would want to proselytize a Jewish neighborhood) a church in Shoreditch that had no vicarage and no local congregation."[12] Ilford was then at the eastern extremity of London. Its own eastern end was still country, though rapidly being developed into row upon row of small "mock-Tudor" houses which she "early learned to despise as jerry-built architectural monstrosities."

Growing up in Ilford as the daughter of a Russian Jewish father who had converted to Christianity and a Welsh mother, there was a part of her that knew she was an outsider:

Among Jews a Goy, among Gentiles (secular or Christian) a Jew or at least a half-Jew (which was good or bad according to their degree of anti-semitism); among Anglo-Saxons a Celt; in Wales a Londoner who not only did not speak Welsh but was not imbued with Welsh attitudes; among school children a strange exception [she was schooled at home] whom they did not know whether to envy or mistrust; all of these anomalies predicated my later experience.[13]

While other children might have found this anomalousness a source of self-doubt and inner confusion, for Levertov, she says, it was just the opposite:

> These feelings of not-belonging were positive for me, not negative. I was given such a sense of confidence by my family, *in* my family, that though I was often shy (and have remained so in certain respects) I nevertheless experienced the sense of difference as an honor, as a part of knowing (secretly) from an early age—perhaps by seven, certainly before I was ten—that I was an artist-person and had a destiny. I did not experience competitiveness, because I was alone. The age gap—nine years—between me and my sister was such that my childhood was largely that of an only child.[14]

Asked to address the questions Who are you? and How did you become what you are? she found that her attempt to answer them increased her awareness of how strong were "inherited tendencies and the influence of the cultural milieu" of her own family. Levertov wrote:

> Father's Hasidic ancestry, his being steeped in Jewish and Christian scholarship and mysticism, his fervor and eloquence as a preacher, were factors built into my cells even though I rarely paid conscious heed to what, as a child, I mostly felt were parts of the embarrassing adult world, and which during my adolescence I rejected as restrictive. Similarly, my mother's Welsh intensity and lyric feeling for Nature were not just the air I breathed but, surely, were in the body I breathed with.[15]

MOTHER: SEEKING A BLESSING

Her mother was a singer. She loved Handel's *Messiah* aria, "I know that my Redeemer liveth," and "despised any performances of it which, though technically excellent, failed to give the emphasis of conviction to that word, 'know': 'I *know* that my Redeemer liveth.'"[16] This illustrates, for Levertov, the fact that her mother's faith was conveyed "more by her tone of voice than by the words she found." We might add that her mother's insistence on a word being rightly emphasized is the kind of subtle parental influence of which poets are made. William Stafford makes a similar point when he says that no great poet influenced him as much as the voice of his mother.[17] In writing a poem, he says, "I find internal resonances rather than traditions of literature. Something of the tonality of my mother's voice . . . recurs to me now;

and I feel the bite of her disappointment in life, and a wry angle of her vision."[18]

Levertov's mother appears in several of her poems. In "Prologue: An Interim," Levertov is concerned with the fate of the soul as the Vietnam War drags on. The language of technical warfare debases language itself, and threatens the soul, which is so dependent on the richness of language for its survival. To "repossess our souls we fly to the sea." She recalls a childhood experience when her mother forgave her:[19]

> At fourteen
> after measles my mother took me
> to stay by the sea. In the austere presence
>
> of Beachy Head we sat long hours
> close to the tideline. She read aloud
> from George Eliot, while I half-dozed
> and played with pebbles. Or I read
> to myself Richard Jeffries'
> *The Story of My Heart*, which begins
> in such majesty.
>   I was mean and grouchy
> much of the time, but she forgave me,
>
> and years later remembered
> only the peace of that time.
>
> The quiet there is
> in listening.
>   Peace could be
>
> that grandeur, that dwelling
> in majestic presence, attuned
> to the great pulse. . . .

Most of Levertov's poems about her mother center on her mother's death and her own desire for her mother's blessing. In "A Daughter (I),"[20] she recognizes that a part of her aches for her mother's pain as the older woman is dying—in Mexico—"far away from home, thousands of miles of earth and sea, and ninety years from her roots." There is another part of herself as well:

the daughter knows
another, hidden part of her longed—or longs—
for her mother to be her mother again,
consoling, judging, forgiving,
whose arms were once
        strong to hold her and rock her,
who used to chant
        a ritual song that did magic
to take away hurt. Now mother is child, helpless; her mind
is clear, her spirit proud, she can even laugh—
but half-blind, half-deaf, and struck down
in body, she's a child in being at the mercy
of looming figures who have the power
to move her, feed her, wash her, leave or stay
at will. And the daughter feels, with horror,
metamorphosed: *she's* such a looming figure—huge—a
                    tower

of iron and ice—love
shrunken in her to a cube of pain
locked in her throat. O, long and long ago
she grew up and went
away and away—and now's bereft
of tears and unable
to comfort the child her mother's become. . . .

Mother and daughter are each unable to give what the other needs, and no other can give: a mother's forgiveness, a daughter's unforced love.

In "A Daughter (II),"[21] written at the same time, she returns to nurse her mother during the last week of dying, but it is now too late for a mother's blessing:

There are flies in the room. The daughter
busies herself, placing wet gauze
over her mother's mouth and eyes.
                What she wants
she knows she can't have: one minute
of communion, here in limbo.

All the years of it,
talk, laughter, letters. Yet something
went unsaid. And there's no place
to put whatever it was, now,
no more chance.

After her mother's death, the forgiveness she sought in life became the subject of her nighttime dreams. In "Visitant"[22] she dreams of her mother's appearance to her and cries or mumbles something about absolution:

From under wide wings of blackest velvet
—a hat such as the Duse might have worn—
peered out at me my mother,
tiny and silver-white, her ancient skin delicately
pink, her eyes their familiar very dark
pebble-green, flecked with amber. "Mother,"
I cried or mumbled, urgent but even now
embarrassed, "can you forgive me? Did you,
as I've feared and feared, feel betrayed
when I failed to be there
at the worse time, and returned
too late? Am I forgiven?" But she looked vague
under the velvet, the ostrich-down, her face small;
if she said mildly, "There is nothing to forgive,"
it seemed likely she wasn't listening,
she was preoccupied with some concerns
of that other life, and when she faded
I was left unabsolved still, the raven drama
of her hat more vivid to me
than she in her polite inattention.
                    This, I told myself,
is fitting: if the dead live
for a while in partial semblances
of their past selves, they have no time
to bear grudges or to bless us;
their own present
holds them intent. Yet perhaps
sometimes they dream us.

As the forgiveness she seeks from her mother is withheld—not because her mother refuses to give it but because she is preoccupied with her own concerns—the pain she feels for a daughter who hoped for a reprise of her mother's "ritual song that did magic to take away hurt" is refocused, and she now weeps tearlessly for the girl that her mother once was. The occasion, related in "A Soul-Cake,"[23] was the reading of her mother's study notes some weeks after her mother's death:

> Mother, when I open a book of yours
> your study notes fall out into my lap.
> "Apse, semicircular or polygonal recess
> arched over domed roof," says one. I remember
> your ceiling, cracked by earthquake,
> and left that way. Not that you chose to leave it;
> nevertheless, "There's nothing less real
> than the present," you underlined.
>
> My throat clenches when I weep and
> can't make tears,
> the way my feet clenched when I ran
> unsuspecting into icy ocean
> for "General swim," visiting Nik at summercamp.
> What hurts is not your absence only,
> dull, unresonant, final,
> it's the intimate knowledge of your aspirations,
> the scholar in you, the artist reaching
> out and out.
>   To strangers your unremitting
> struggle to learn appears
> to triumph—to me, poignant. I know
> how baffled you felt.
> I know only I
> knew how lonely you were.
> The small orphan,
> skinny, proud, reserved, observant,
> irreverent still in the woman of ninety,
> but humble.

"To force conscience," you marked in Panofsky,
"is worse,' says Castellio, 'than cruelly
to kill a man. For to deny one's convictions
destroys the soul."

          And Bruno's lines,
"The age
Which I have lived, live, and shall live,
Sets me atremble, shakes, and braces me."

Five months before you died you recalled
counting-rhymes, dance-games for me;
gaily, under the moon, you sang and mimed,

> My shoes are very *dirty*,
> My shoes are very *thin*,
> I haven't got a *pocket*
> To put a penny in.

> A *soul-cake, a soul-cake,*
> *Please, good missis, a soul-cake* . . .

But by then for two years
you had hardly been able to hear me,
could barely see to read.
          We spoke together
          less and less.

There's too much grief. Mother,
what shall I do with it?
Salt grinding and grinding from the magic box.

So there will be no maternal blessing, no absolution. But through the experience of her mother's death she not only sees her mother's decline into a helpless child but also comes to know her mother *as a child,* and it is this child, who lived in her mother's adult body, to whom she is able to reach out. It is this child whom she had understood: the aspirations that only her daughter was to fulfill, and the loneliness, which only her daughter had seen. It is as though the child in her mother—the small skinny orphan—was the only one who could give a blessing, and through *her* own writings—the study notes of a woman of ninety—she did.

FATHER: CONVEYING A DAUGHTER'S LOVE

In poems about her father, Levertov stresses his boldness. Like her mother, he too was a student, but his studies led him to a discovery that caused his family to laugh and then to weep. "Wings in the Pedlar's Pack" is written with marginal glosses reminiscent of rabbinical lore:[24]

The certainty of wings: a child's bold heart,
not, good little *Schul*-boy, Torah or Talmud
gave it to you, a practical vision:
wings were needed, why should people
plod forever on foot, not glide like herons
through the blue and white
promise unfolding
over their heads, over
the river's thawing?
Therefore the pedlar. (But why did they not
avail themselves of his wares?)

> My father, as a child, sees the magic pedlar Marc Chagall was also to see a few years later. The one intuited that he carried wings, the other painted him, wingless but floating high over Vitepsk.

Later, *ochetz moy*, when you discovered
wings for your soul, the same bold heart
empowered you. From Prussia east and
   southward
verst after *verst* you willed the train to go
          faster,
skimming the rails home to the Dnieper valley.
You bore such news, so longed-for,
fulfilling a hope so ancient
it had almost become dry parchment,
          not hope any more.
At the station you hailed a *droshky*,
greeted the driver like a brother. At last
there was the street, there was the house:
but when you arrived
they would not listen.
They laughed at you. And then they wept.
But would not listen.

> My father, as a student, discovers the Messiah,

> and hurries home with the good news,

> but is not believed.

In "Perhaps No Poem But All I Can Say And I Can't Be Silent," which is about how her parents could not have borne the current "Age of Terror," she describes her father as "a devout Christian" who "took delight and pride in being (like Christ and the Apostles) a Jew," but who also drew on his heritage, Hasidic lore, "to know the Holy Spirit as Shekinah." (In the same poem, she recalls that her mother had "cherished all her long life the words of Israel Zangwill, who told her, 'You have a Jewish soul.' ")[25]

A recent poem, "The Opportunity," parallels her earlier poem, "The Soul-Cake," though here it is not her ninety-year-old mother's study notes, but a dream, that is the means by which she embraces the "child" of her father:[26]

My father once, after his death,
appeared to me as a rose,
passed beyond intellect.
This time, he resumes
human form to become
a boy of six.
I kneel to hug him,
kiss the child's bare shoulder;
near us the ocean
sighs and murmurs,
firm sand reflects
the turn of the wave.

This is my chance to tell him,
"Much has happened, over the years,
many travels.
In the world,
in myself.
Along the way,
I have come to believe
the truth of what you believe."

The child, with good grace,
permits
my brief embrace; he smiles:
the words
are lazy waves above and around him,

he absorbs their tone,
knows he is loved.
Knows only that.

This was my chance
to speak, I've taken it,
we are both content.

The relationship between them is not one in which blessing is sought and withheld. What matters is that he knows she loves him, and she is confident of that.

SISTER: SEARCH FOR THE EVERLASTING ARMS

In her autobiographical sketch Levertov notes that her sister, Olga, was nine years older than she, and that her own childhood was consequently largely that of an only child. Yet Olga was very much a part of her life and an important presence in the family. Concerned that she may be accused of having idealized her childhood in what she had written about it, Denise acknowledges, "There were also tremendous domestic arguments and periodic fullscale 'rows' and even real tragedy (my gifted but erratic sister's life and her conflicts and reconciliations with my parents were complex)."[27]

Olga, who died in 1964 at age fifty, has been the subject of several poems by her younger sister. Like Stafford's poems on his brother, Bob, they focus on Denise's sense that her sister was a victim in life, as though she and the world were never able to come to terms with one another. In demeanor, though, Olga was more like Stafford's sister, Peg, the soldierly one.

The first of her poems entitled "Olga Poems"[28] was written two months after her sister's death. Olga is portrayed here as the sister who was deeply attuned to the world's injustice:

You wanted
to shout the world to its senses,
did you?—to browbeat

the poor into joy's
socialist republic—
What rage

and human shame swept you
when you were nine and saw
the Ley Street houses,

grasping their meaning as *slum*.
Where I, reaching that age,
teased you, admiring

architectural probity, circa
eighteen-fifty, and noted
pride in the whitened doorsteps.

Black one, black one,
there was a white
candle in your heart.

As the poem continues, Levertov is critical of her sister's "rage for order" and the problems this created for others:[29]

But dread
was in her, a bloodbeat, it was against the rolling dark
oncoming river she raised bulwarks, setting herself
to sift cinders after early Mass all of one winter,

labelling her desk's normal disorder, basing
her verses on Keble's *Christian Year*, picking
those endless arguments, pressing on

to manipulate lives to disaster . . . To change,
to change the course of the river! What rage for order
disordered her pilgrimage—so that for years at a time

she would hide among strangers, waiting
to rearrange all mysteries in a new light.

When Olga lay dying, it was as if she had burned herself out, and nothing was left of her rage, it having been replaced by the single white candle burning in her heart:[30]

On your hospital bed you lay
in love, the hatreds

117

that had followed you, a
comet's tail, burned out

as your disasters bred of love
burned out,
while pain and drugs
quarreled like sisters in you—

lay afloat on a sea
of love and pain—how you always
loved that cadence, "Underneath
are the everlasting arms"—

all history
burned out, down
to the sick bone, save for

that kind candle.

As the "Olga Poems" draw to a conclusion, she recalls a photo of her older sister, taken when Olga was three, and she remembers her sister's eyes, and "the fear in them":[31]

What did you do with your fear,
later? Through the years of humiliation,
of paranoia and blackmail and near-starvation, losing
the love of those you loved, one after another,
parents, lovers, children, idolized friends, what kept
compassion's candle alight in you.
. . . .

I cross
so many brooks in the world, there is so much light
dancing on so many stones, so many questions my eyes
smart to ask of your eyes, gold brown eyes,
the lashes short but the lids
arched as if carved out of olivewood, eyes with some vision
of festive goodness in back of their hard, or veiled, or shining,
unknowable gaze. . . .

118

Some twenty years later she wrote again of Olga, in "To Olga," stressing again her sister's lack of self-trust and the fear of the world in her eyes:[32]

When the last sunlight had all seeped
down behind the woods and taken
colors and shadows with it, leaving us
not in darkness but in
the presence of an absence, with everything
still visible but
empty of soul—

when we trudged on knowing our home was
miles and hours away and the real dark
overtaking us, and mother and father waiting
anxious by now and soon
growing angry because again
we'd traveled too far out and away, leaving
almost as if
not to return—

what did you, almost grown up, feel
as we spoke less and less, too tired
for fantasy? I was afraid for them,
for their fear and of
its show of anger, but not of the night.
I felt the veil
of sadness descend

but I was never afraid for us,
we were benighted but not lost, and I trusted
utterly that at last,
however late, we'd get home.
No owl, no lights, the dun ridges
of ploughland fading. No matter.
I trusted you.

But you? Irritably you'd ask me
why I was silent. Was it because
you felt untrusted, or had no trust

in yourself? Could it,
could it have been that
you, you were afraid,
my brave, my lost
sister?

In a recent poem entitled "Suspended,"[33] she again recalls Olga's love of that cadence "Underneath are the everlasting arms" and claims it now for herself:

I had grasped God's garment in the void
but my hand slipped
on the rich silk of it.
The "everlasting arms" my sister loved to remember
must have upheld my leaden weight
from falling, even so,
for though I claw at empty air and feel
nothing, no embrace,
I have not plummetted.

She has experienced the "everlasting arms" that her sister—so bereft of trust—had longed to experience for herself. This, too, is the language of the body, and reminiscent of her own desire for longer arms that could wrap another, like vines, fourfold. But now the arms are there for her, not in the form of an embrace, but as upholding arms, protecting her from free-falling out of this world of ours.

For Levertov, the neighborhood of Ilford or the community of poets in America were not particularly important in the forming of her vocation as a poet. The dominant influence was "the cultural milieu" of her own family. It was in this crucible—involving her mother, her father, her sister, and her own sense of being "an only child"—that her vocation took seed and grew. Over against the domestic arguments and her sister's combativeness, she developed "an appreciation of solitude."[34] It was because her sister's one year at a convent boarding school had not gone well for her that their mother had decided to keep Denise at home. From her family, *in* her family, she gained a great "sense of confidence." But home was also the place she sought refuge *from,* and she "was given a great deal of freedom to roam about outdoors as soon as [she'd] learned to cross streets safely; only the loneliest depths of Wanstead Park were out of bounds."[35] Is it any wonder that she sees herself in

"Judy," the student who "set off alone, winter nights, coat collar up, and in your pocket that invisible flute"? If Olga would long for the "everlasting arms," Denise would be drawn and won by the cadence of "the peace that passeth all understanding."[36]

". . . That Passeth All Understanding"

An awe so quiet
I don't know when it began.

A gratitude
had begun
to sing in me.

Was there
some moment
dividing
song from no song?

When does dewfall begin?

When does night
fold its arms over our hearts
to cherish them?

When is daybreak?

THE EXPERIENCE OF WOMANHOOD

SO MUCH IS UNFOLDING

One of the things I most appreciate about Denise Levertov's poetry is that what she says about herself as a woman could be said about most other women, and when she writes about women in general her own experiences are unmistakably present. Her poems that concern the experiences of women reflect the truth of Carl Rogers's observation that what is most personal is most general or universal. There have been times, he writes,

> when in talking with students or staff, or in my writing, I have expressed myself in ways so personal that I have felt I was expressing an attitude which it was probable no one else could understand, because it was so

uniquely my own. . . . In these instances I have almost invariably found that the very feeling which has seemed to me most private, most personal, and hence most incomprehensible by others, has turned out to be an expression for which there is a resonance in many other people. It has led me to believe that what is most personal and unique in each of us is probably the very element which would, if it were shared or expressed, speak most deeply to others. This has helped me to understand artists and poets who have dared to express the unique in themselves.[37]

Thus, as we explore Levertov's poems that concern women's experience, I will not separate those that are self-referential from those that speak about women in general.

Several of her poems focus on a woman's experience of being in process or transition, and of being comfortable with her in-betweenness. In "Stepping Westward," she asserts, "If woman is inconstant, good, I am faithful to ebb and flow, I fall in season and now is a time of ripening."[38] In "July 1968"[39] she describes herself as "not young, and not yet old":

> Topmost leaves of young oak,
>   young maple,
>   are red—a delicate red
> almost maroon.
>
> I am not young,
>   and not yet old. Young enough not to be able
>   to imagine my own old age. Something in me
>
> puts out new leaves that are red also,
>   delicate, fantastic, in June,
>   early summer, late spring in the north.
>
> A dark time we live in. One would think
>   there would be no summer. No red leaves.
>   One would think there would be
>
> no drawings-up of the blind at morning
>   to a field awake with flowers.
>   Yet with my tuft of new leaves
>
> it is that field I wake to,
>   a woman foolish with desire.

Perhaps it is her "foolish desire" that keeps her in process, that causes her always to "put out new leaves."

Similarly, in "I learned that her name was Proverb,"[40] she speaks of being led or drawn into a labyrinth of twisting valleys and steeper mountains:

> And the secret names
> of all we meet who lead us deeper
> into our labyrinth
> of valleys and mountains, twisting valleys
> and steeper mountains—
> their hidden names are always,
> like Proverb, promises:
> Rune, Omen, Fable, Parable,
> those we meet for only
> one crucial moment, gaze to gaze,
> or for years know and don't recognize
>
> but of whom later a word
> sings back to us
> as if from high among leaves,
> still near but beyond sight
>
> drawing us from tree to tree
> towards the time and the unknown place
> where we shall know
> what it is to arrive.

Eventually women will know what it is to arrive, but for now their experience is that of being drawn forward by irresistible promises.

If a woman is in process and cannot say that she has arrived, so much of her life is spent in finding ways to keep her hopes up, especially when it would be so easy to give in to despair. In "Beginners,"[41] the fact that there is so much that needs to be done is grounds for hope:

> *"From too much love of living,*
> *Hope and desire set free,*
> *Even the weariest river*
> *Winds somewhere to the sea—"*

But we have only begun
to love the earth.

We have only begun
to imagine the fulness of life.

How could we tire of hope?
—so much is in bud.

How can desire fail?
—we have only begun
to imagine justice and mercy,
only begun to envision

how it might be
to live as siblings with beast and flower,
not as oppressors.

Surely our river
cannot already be hastening
into the sea of nonbeing?

Surely it cannot
drag, in the silt,
all that is innocent?

Not yet, not yet—
there is too much broken
that must be mended,

too much hurt we have done to each other
that cannot yet be forgiven.

We have only begun to know
the power that is in us if we would join
our solitudes in the communion of struggle.

So much is unfolding that must
complete its gesture,

so much is in bud.

MORE FEARFUL FOR OTHERS, MORE DAUNTLESS FOR SELF

Hoping is what any of us might do to cope with our fears and anxieties. In "Hoping,"[42] she suggests, ruefully, almost ironically, that this is what she tries to do when there seems to be nothing in life that reassures:

> All my life hoping the nightmare
> I dreamed as a child (and could make recur
> if perverse fascination willed it)
> was not prophetic:
>   all the animals
> seated in peaceful council by candleglow
> in a shadowy, fragrant barn,
> timeless, unmenaced—then without warning,
> without any flash or noise,
> the crumbling to black ash, ash
> corrugated, writhing, as filmy shreds
> of paper used to when sheets of it,
> place round the firescreen to coax the draft
> upward and liven the coals, would themselves
> catch fire and float, newsprint curdling,
> dreadfully out from the hearth towards me.
> All my life hoping; having to hope
> because decades brought no reassurance.

Prominent among a woman's fears is the threat that life poses for those she loves. In "Abel's Bride"[43] the woman, stronger, even more mature than the man, is left to worry for him as he goes out on his solitary quests:

> Woman fears for man, he goes
> out alone to his labors. No mirror
> nests in his pocket. His face
> opens and shuts with his hopes.
> His sex hangs unhidden
> or rises before him
> blind and questing.

She thinks herself
lucky. But sad. When she goes out
she looks in the glass, she remembers
herself. Stones, coal,
the hiss of water upon the kindled
branches—her being
is a cave, there are bones at the hearth.

In "During a Son's Dangerous Illness"[44] she struggles with her worst dread, the possibility that her son could die tragically before her:

You could die before me—
I've known it
always, the
dreaded worst, "unnatural" but
possible
in the play
of matter, matter and
growth and
fate.

•

My sister Philippa died
twelve years before I was born—
the perfect, laughing firstborn,
a gift to be cherished as my orphaned mother
had not been cherished. Suddenly:
death, a baby

cold and still.

•

Parent, child—death ignores
protocol, a sweep of its cape brushes
this one or that one at random
into the dust, it was
not even looking.

What becomes
of the past if the future
snaps off, brittle,
the present left as a jagged edge
opening on nothing?

.

Grief for the menaced world—lost rivers,
poisoned lakes—all creatures, perhaps,
to be fireblasted
              off the
whirling cinder we
loved, but not enough . . .
The grief I'd know if I
lived into
your unthinkable death
is a splinter
of that selfsame grief,
infinitely smaller but
the same in kind:
one
stretching the mind's fibers to touch
eternal nothingness,
the other
tasting, in fear, the
desolation of
survival.

While the death of her child before her own would be so devastatingly
"unnatural," the woman has a strong presentiment—as though it is her fate in
life—of being preceded in death by the man. In "Stele,"[45] a memorial to the
dead, he leads the way into the shades, their separation increasing as they pass
deeper and deeper into the afterlife:

They part at the edge of substance.
Henceforth, he will be shadow
in a land of shadow.
And she—she too will be going

slowly down a road of cloud,
weightless, untouched, untouching.
This is the last crossroad.
Her right hand and his left
are clasped, but already,
muffled in his acceptance of fate,
his attention recedes from her.
Her left hand rises, fingertips trace
the curve of his warm face
as it cools and fades.
He has looked down his road,
he is ready to go, not willingly
yet without useless resistance.
She too accepts the truth, there is no way back,
but she has not looked, yet, at the path
accorded to her. She has not given herself,
not yet, to her shadowhood.

Experiencing the loss of persons who were once close to us is not exclusive to women, yet in "The Passing Bell"[46] it seems fitting that it is an old woman who is left to register their passing:

One by one
they fall away—

all whom they really
wanted to keep. People.
Things that were more than things.

The dog, the cat,
the doll with a silk dress,
the red penknife:
those were the first to go.

Then father, mother,
sister, brother,
wife and husband.
Now the child.

The child is grown,
the child is gone,

the child has said,
Don't touch me, don't call me,

your lights have gone out,
I don't love you.
No more.

The distant child
casts a tall shadow:
that's the dark.
And they are small.

The world is brittle,
seamed with cracks,
ready to shatter. Now

the old man steps
into a boat,
rows down the rainy street.
Old woman, she climbs up

into the steeple's eye.
Transmogrified, she's
the clapper of the bell.

The tolling begins.

While a woman's fears are especially associated with the threat that life poses for those she cares deeply about, a woman also has fears for herself. Yet "A Woman Alone"[47] is a bracing word for those who have fears of aging:

She has fears, but not about loneliness;
fears about how to deal with the aging
of her body—how to deal
with photographs and the mirror. She feels
so much younger and more beautiful
than she looks. At her happiest
—or even in the midst of
some less than joyful hour, sweating
patiently through a heatwave in the city
or hearing the sparrows at daybreak, dully gray,
toneless, the sound of fatigue—

a kind of sober euphoria makes her believe
in her future as an old woman, a wanderer,
seamed and brown,
little luxuries of the middle of life all gone,
watching cities and rivers, people and mountains,
without being watched; not grim nor sad.

. . . .

Now at least
she is past the time of mourning,
now she can say without shame or deceit,
O blessed Solitude.

While afraid of pain, Levertov asserts that she does not fear death. Therefore in "The Emissary"[48] she declares that she will not sit still while death's emissary goes about spreading her chill on women who want to experience life to the full:

Twice now this woman for whom my unreasonable dislike
has slowly turned to loathing
has come up to me and said, "Ah, yes,
we shall have plenty of time soon to talk."

Twice she has laid her cold hand heavily
on mine,
and thrust her pallid face, her puffy cheeks,
close to mine.
I went to wash in the hottest water, to oil myself
in fragrant oils.

I know who she is in the world; others know her;
many seem not to notice she brings
a chill into rooms.
She is who she is,
ordinary, venal, perhaps sad.
Perhaps she is not aware of her own task:
but death sends her about the world.

I have always been afraid of pain
but not of death.
I am not afraid of death, but I don't want

to have time
to sit and talk with this woman.

I have watched her condescend
to those who don't know her name,
and smirk at the ones who do.
I have seen her signature
hiding under pebbles,
scratched into chips of ice.

She can have nothing to tell me
I could be glad to hear.

PROFILES IN COURAGE

It is often a woman's fate to experience defeat and, more often than not, to be left to ponder her defeats alone, without the support or commiseration of others. "A Defeat in the Green Mountains"[49] is a poignant account of a woman who meets with unanticipated obstacles and is forced to give up:

On a dull day she goes
to find the river,
accompanied by two
unwilling children, shut in
among thorns, vines, the
long grass

stumbling, complaining, the
blackflies biting them,
but persists, drawn
by river-sound close beyond
the baffling scratchy thicket

and after a half-hour they emerge
upon the water
            flowing by
both dark and clear.
        A space and
        a movement crossing
        their halted movement.
But the river is deep

the mud her foot stirs up
frightens her; the kids are
scared and angry. No way
to reach the open fields over there.
Back then:
swamp underfoot, through the

perverse thickets, finding
a path finally to the
main road—defeated,
to ponder the narrow
depth of the river,
its absorbed movement past her.

The obstacles that are placed in front of women—many "foolish with desire"—are baffling and perplexing. They would seem not to be insurmountable, and yet they so often are.

On the other hand, Levertov writes eloquently about women who struggle against great odds. She invites us to listen attentively to the stories of women's lives, for when we do, we gain a deep sense that women are living profiles in courage. Her poem on the annunciation declares that Mary was free "to accept or to refuse, choice integral to humanness," and that she willingly accepted her destiny:[50]

She did not cry, "I cannot, I am not worthy,"
nor, "I have not the strength."
She did not submit with gritted teeth,
                      raging, coerced.
Bravest of all humans,
            consent illumined her.
The room filled with its light,
the lily glowed in it,
            and the iridescent wings.

Consent,
      courage unparalleled,
opened her utterly.

In the same way, for us,

> Aren't there annunciations
> of one sort or another
> in most lives?
>> Some unwillingly
> undertake great destinies,
> enact them in sullen pride,
> uncomprehending.
>> More often
> those moments
>> when roads of light and storm
>>> open from darkness in a man or woman,
> are turned away from
> in dread, in a wave of weakness, in despair
> and with relief.
> Ordinary lives continue.
>>>> God does not smite them.
> But the gates close, the pathway vanishes.

So it was a young woman—Mary—who was the very exemplar of courage, the courage called for in "those moments when roads of light and storm open from darkness in a man or woman," and we are free to accept or to refuse. If we are accustomed to think of men as the courageous ones, Levertov helps us to see that those who have the greatest reason to fear—the women—are those of whom courage is most often required. Typically, this is the courage of consent: I accept the challenge that has been placed before me.

"HER UNDERSTANDING KEEPS ON TRANSLATING"

An important theme in Levertov's work, and an important issue for pastors who are concerned to hear the voices of women, is the role that men play in women's lives. She takes keen interest in the attempt of men and women to relate to one another in spite of their obvious differences. In "The Mutes,"[51] she explores the conflicted feelings that attention from men evoke in women:

Those groans men use
passing a woman on the street
or on the steps of the subway

to tell her she is a female
and their flesh knows it,

are they a sort of tune,
an ugly enough song, sung
by a bird with a slit tongue

but meant for music?

Or are they the muffled roaring
of deafmutes trapped in a building that is
slowly filling with smoke?

Perhaps both.

Such men most often
look as if groan were all they could do,
yet a woman, in spite of herself,

knows it's a tribute:
if she were lacking all grace
they'd pass her in silence:

so it's not only to say she's
a warm hole. It's a word

in grief-language, nothing to do with
primitive, not an ur-language;
language stricken, sickened, cast down

in decrepitude. She wants to
throw the tribute away, dis-
gusted, and can't,

it goes on buzzing in her ear,
it changes the pace of her walk,
the torn posters in echoing corridors

spell it out, it
quakes and gnashes as the train comes in.
Her pulse sullenly

> had picked up speed,
> but the cars slow down and
> jar to a stop while her understanding
>
> keeps on translating:
> "Life after life after life goes by
>
> without poetry,
> without seemliness,
> without love."

This poem indicates that women frequently do not trust their responses to men, that their encounters with men force them to question themselves and to ponder the very meaning of their lives. This is a power that men have over women that women often resent.

In another poem "To R.D., March 4th 1988," Levertov focuses on a dream she had of her own mentor, from whom she had long since been estranged. Here, as in the preceding poem, the woman finds herself pondering the meaning that a relationship to a man has for her own self-understanding:[52]

> You were my mentor. Without knowing it,
> I outgrew the need for a mentor.
> Without knowing it, you resented that,
> and attacked me. I bitterly resented
> the attack, and without knowing it
> freed myself to move forward
> without a mentor. Love and long friendship
> corroded, shrank, and vanished from sight
> into some underlayer of being.
> The years rose and fell, rose and fell,
> and the news of your death after years of illness
> was a fact without resonance for me,
> I had lost you long before, and mourned you,
> and put you away like a folded cloth
> put away in a drawer. But today I woke
> while it was dark, from a dream
> that brought you live into my life:
> I was in a church, near the Lady Chapel
> at the head of the west aisle. Hearing a step
> I turned: you were about to enter

the row behind me, but our eyes met
and you smiled at me, your unfocused eyes
focussing in that smile to renew
all the reality our foolish pride extinguished.
You moved past me then, and as you sat down
beside me, I put a welcoming hand
over yours, and your hand was warm.
I had no need
for a mentor, nor you to be one;
but I was once more
your chosen sister, and you
my chosen brother.
We heard strong harmonies rise and begin to fill
the arching stone,
sounds that had risen here through centuries.

Her understanding of her relationship to this particular man undergoes a series of translations. At first, he was her mentor, a man on whom she leaned at that critical period in her life when she was becoming established in her chosen vocation. But when she outgrew her need for a mentor without realizing it, he became her attacker, which, while painful to her, also freed her to move forward without him. Now, after his death, she finds she is unable to mourn, because she had already mourned her loss of him years ago. This does not, however, conclude the process of translation, for in her dream she experiences him as her chosen brother and she his chosen sister. As she had grown up without a brother, the fact that he could be received as brother is important, for it was this role that he filled all the while that he was also mentor to her, and it is the fact that he was brother to her that survives. They sit together in the church, hands touching, listening to the strong harmonies that rise and begin to fill the arching stone. Unlike birth siblings, they have chosen each other.

If this poem speaks about the freedom Levertov gained once "R.D." began to attack her, several of her poems focus on the fact that, for women generally, nothing good comes from men's attacks against them. "The Batterers"[53] focuses on the emotions that are evoked in a man who has just subjected a woman to a violent beating:

A man sits by the bed
of a woman he has beaten,

dresses her wounds,
gingerly dabs at bruises.
Her blood pools about her,
darkens.

Astonished, he finds he's begun
to cherish her. He is terrified.
Why had he never
seen, before, what she was?
What if she stops breathing?

Earth, can we not love you
unless we believe the end is near?
Believe in your life
unless we think you are dying?

For Levertov, men's attacks on women are symptomatic of their attitudes toward the earth itself, which they have brutalized and left for dead over and over again. In "Urgent Whisper,"[54] she tells how she has begun to feel in her own bones this brutalization of the woman named Earth, causing her to shudder and tremble:

It could be the râle of Earth's tight chest,
her lungs scarred from old fevers, and she asleep—

but there's no news from the seismographs,
the crystal pendant
hangs plumb from its hook;

and yet at times (and I whisper because
it's a fearful thing I tell you)
a subtle shudder has passed
from outside me into my bones,

up from the ground beneath me,
beneath this house, beneath
the road and the trees:

a silent delicate trembling no one has spoken of,
as if a beaten child or a captive animal
lay waiting the next blow.

It comes from the Earth herself, I tell you,
Earth herself. I whisper
because I'm ashamed. Isn't the earth our mother?
Isn't it we who've brought
this terror upon her?

These brutalities against Earth are beyond a woman's understanding. She views them uncomprehendingly. It is not that she is confused by them, or uncertain about her reaction to them. They are unspeakable acts, and what is especially infuriating to her is that men obscure the brutality of these acts through a degradation of the very language that, in her own experience as a poet, has given of itself so willingly and unreservedly: a language of consent. "Misnomer"[55] focuses on men's association of their unspeakable acts to art:

They speak of the art of war,
but the arts
draw their light from the soul's well,
and warfare
dries up the soul and draws its power
from a dark and burning wasteland.
When Leonardo
set his genius to devising
machines of destruction he was not
acting in the service of art,
he was suspending
the life of art
over an abyss,
as if one were to hold
a living child out of an airplane window
at thirty thousand feet.

In a "political poem" protesting the Persian Gulf War in 1991 entitled "Witnessing from Afar the New Escalation of Savage Power,"[56] Levertov complains that the wars that men plan and execute are an assault on a woman's spirit, even an old woman who had lived through several wars and thought she had seen every atrocity of man's devising:

She was getting old, had seen a lot,
knew a lot.

But something innocent
enlivened her,
upheld her spirits.
She tended a small altar,
kept a candle shielded there,
or tried to. There was a crash and throb
of harsh sound audible
always, but distant.
She believed
she had it in her
to fend for herself and hold
despair at bay.
Now when she came to the ridge and saw
the world's raw gash
reopened, the whole world
a valley of steaming blood,
her small wisdom
guttered in the uprush;
rubbledust, meatpulse—
darkness and the blast
levelled her. (Not her own death,
that was not yet.) The deafening
downrush. Shock, shame
no memory, no knowledge
nor dark imagination
had prepared her for.

If men are about the "escalation" of savage power, Levertov—a woman of spirit—has dedicated her life to the transforming power of language. In a section of "A Common Ground" introduced by a quotation from the Russian poet Boris Pasternak—"everything in the world must excel itself to be itself"—she speaks about language that brings not darkness and despair but light and song:[57]

Not "common speech"
a dead level
but the uncommon speech of paradise,
tongue in which oracles
speak to beggars and pilgrims:

not illusion but what Whitman called
"the path
between reality and the soul,"
a language
excelling itself to be itself,

speech akin to the light
with which at day's end and day's
renewal, mountains
sing to each other across the cold valleys.

Similarly, in "The Acolyte,"[58] she writes about the woman who uses words to "break evil spells":

The large kitchen is almost dark.
Across the plain of even, diffused light,
copper pans on the wall and the window geranium
tend separate campfires.
Herbs dangle their Spanish moss from rafters.

At the table, floury hands
kneading dough, feet planted
steady on flagstones,
a woman ponders the loaves-to-be.
Yeast and flour, water and salt,
have met in the huge bowl.

It's not
the baked and cooled and cut
bread she's thinking of,
but the way
the dough rises and has a life of its own,

not the oven she's thinking of
but the way
the sour smell changes
to fragrance.

She wants to put
a silver rose or a bell of diamonds
into each loaf;

she wants
to bake a curse into one loaf,
into another, the words that break
evil spells and release
transformed heroes into their selves;
she wants to make
bread that is more than bread.

To be a woman, then, means to be fated to a lifelong, personal struggle with matters of understanding: for self-understanding that is gained in struggling with the confusing mixture of reactions and responses that relations with men evoke in her; for the absolute refusal to "understand" men's brutality toward women and Earth; and for "the peace that passeth all understanding," when a woman, in her solitude, feels "an awe so quiet I don't know when it began."[59]

THE HEARING BARRIER

In a practicum in client-centered therapy when I was a graduate student, the instructor, John Butler, one of Carl Rogers's own students, played two audio tapes involving the same counselee, a woman who was having marital problems. One tape was from a session early in the counseling process, and the other was from a session late in the process. The difference in her ability to speak was dramatic. If we had not been told that she was the same woman, we would never have guessed. As Butler pointed out, she had been helped with her marital problems through therapy, but, more importantly, she had acquired the capacity to speak about and for herself. She had acquired a language expressive of her own inner experience.

I thought of this woman as I read what the counselor had to say in the case of Dorothy, especially his assertion that she was inarticulate and dumb. Then, I reread the case material and took note of the numerous statements of his which were intimidating, making it difficult for her to speak for and about herself. His question early in the session, "Did I catch you saying?" implies that she is on trial, that anything she says may be held against her. He suggests that she cannot hear what her husband is trying to tell her—"So what does that mean? What is he saying?"—he questions her motives for coming to see him—"So you didn't just come to get some things off your chest? You really want to do some hard thinking about how to rebuild this marriage?"—and he virtually compels her to make a personal confession of guilt:

141

Counselor: Do you feel that you have in any way contributed to the problems?
Dorothy: Well, I think he wasn't satisfied with what I would do. You know,
              he wasn't satisfied. He was always complaining about what I was
              doing—the way I did things. So I guess that I was contributing.

Thus, in going to see the pastoral counselor, Dorothy encountered another man besides her husband who was not satisfied with how she presented herself, with how she reflected upon her problems, and with her slowness to acknowledge her personal responsibility for the problems in her marriage. Instead of being affirmed, instead of having her view that her husband simply didn't love her taken seriously, she was confronted by a pastoral counselor who aligned himself on the side of her husband, and, in his post-session interpretation, directly blamed her for "lousing up" her marriage.

As Justes points out, a counselor who had broken free of stereotypical attitudes toward women would have been able to see that:

> The primary goal for Dorothy might not be that she continue in the marriage, but that she be able to break patterns of dependency and come to be in charge of her own life; not that she live irresponsibly in relationships with others, but that she live with some responsibility for herself and her decisions, having awareness of her feelings and assurance of her self-worth. What a different outcome for Dorothy would result from work with a pastoral counselor who would not hold her bound to a stereotype of what woman should be![60]

Hearing the voice of the other is not merely a matter of casting our nets wider, so as to create a more socially and culturally diverse clientele for our ministries of pastoral care and counseling. Of course, efforts to reach out to those who are different from us in terms of race, sexual orientation, social class, and age are essential. As David W. Augsburger points out in *Pastoral Counseling Across Cultures*:

> The time has come for the pastoral counseling movement to function from an expanded, intercultural perspective. The counseling theories and therapies that have emerged as modes of healing and growth in each culture, useful and effective as they are in their respective locales, are too limited, too partial to serve human needs in a world community where peoples of many cultures meet, compete, and relate.[61]

Yet are we not being rather presumptuous in these efforts to widen our horizons when we have been unable to hear the voices in our very own midst? What good will it do for us to widen our horizons if we continue to brutalize the women in our midst by the way we talk down to them? Also, as Levertov shows, if it is we men who have not yet learned the transforming power of language, there are also women who, like the woman in "The Emissary," have nothing to tell other women that they could be glad to hear. Let us all begin to make bread that is more than bread. Let us all learn to speak to one another in a language that excels itself to be itself.

We must learn truly to listen to the voice of the other, to empty our minds and hearts of all preconceptions, prejudices, and predictions, and to hear:

Dorothy: I . . . still love him but I can't live with him.
Counselor: Would you care to tell me why?
Dorothy: Ah—because he doesn't care about me.
Counselor: Ummm, you don't feel that he loves you?
Dorothy: No. I don't think he ever did.

This is a woman who believes her husband doesn't care for her, and never really loved her. What a sad and tragic realization! Unloved, un-cared about, she is bereft and despairing, hurt, frustrated, and angry. If her counselor could hear, he would know that she *had* come precisely to "get some things off her chest"—to find some relief for the pressure, constriction, and pain of a breaking heart. She came because she was seeking the everlasting arms—if not to embrace her, then at least to uphold her leaden weight from falling. She came seeking a pastor of grief and dreams of whom it might be said, "How beautiful his patience" as he accompanies her across the river of her defeat to the open spaces beyond: where she may hear her inner voice inviting her consent to even greater courage.

5. Pastoral Care and the Yearning for Freedom

I N *The Presence of God in Pastoral Counseling*, Wayne E. Oates looks
back on his fifty years as a pastoral counselor, and recognizes that his
"concern for the Presence of God in a trialogue with counselees" has
been "the living heart of my work."[1] From personal experience, he is able to
say that

> the pastoral counselor who accepts the quest for the Presence of God as
> the central focus of his or her counseling will have a *lasting* center, one
> that lives on past the threat of condemnation, the threat of meaningless-
> ness, and the threat of aging and death.[2]

He hastens to assure his reader that

> I have not come to this realization in a momentary enthusiasm nor out of
> a desire to seem more or less pious than I am. Over the years, my most
> significant memories in pastoral counseling have been in those spiritual
> breakthroughs when the Presence of God became intensely evident
> without contrivance or technique on my part and much to the awe-struck
> amazement on both the counselee's and my part.[3]

He cites the several editions of his book *The Christian Pastor* as evidence of
his continuous attention to the issue of the presence of God, and of the
different but compatible ways in which he articulated it:

> In the first edition, I centered pastoral care and counseling in the pastor's
> representation of God's Presence at times of crisis. In the second edition,
> I focused our work on the identity and integrity of the pastor as a "teacher

come from God." In the 1982 edition, I concentrated on the pastor's participation in the wisdom or counsel of God in the exercise of the gift of discernment. The pastor is a *tebunah*, a person of understanding (Proverbs 20:5).[4]

In his recent book, *Prayer in Pastoral Counseling*, Edward P. Wimberly expresses a similar conviction regarding the healing presence of God in the ministry of pastoral counseling, and he, too, concentrates on the pastor's participation in the wisdom or counsel of God in the exercise of the gift of discernment. For Wimberly, the central task of the pastoral counselor is to focus attention on discerning where and how God is at work in the lives of those who have come for help. The primary way this is done is through prayer at the conclusion of the counseling session. In a prayer offered as a marriage counseling session was coming to a close, Wimberly said these words:

> We request your guidance this day on the problem of religious differences that Karen and Ralph have expressed. We sense the urgency that they feel about this issue. We also feel the helplessness that they feel in finding ways to resolve this problem. Reveal to them and to me where you are at work helping them to bring resolution to this problem.[5]

Here is an explicit request for insight into how God is already working in their lives, together with a clearly expressed promise to do all in their power to work alongside God toward the solution of their marital problems.

Oates is also concerned in his book with the issue of how God is to be understood. What is the nature of the God who is present in the counseling moment? For him, two biblical metaphors of the presence of God are especially important. Both are relational metaphors. One is the metaphor of the "face" of God which emphasizes the overwhelming difference between us and God:

> We cannot survive in the contrast. Our "over-againstness" as we stand in the Presence of God rocks the things in our lives which can be shaken in order that the things which cannot be moved may remain. The positive, conjunctive emotions associated with such an encounter with God are reverence, awe, and a desire to please God above all others. When we are alienated from God, these feelings turn into terror, a fear of punishment, a suspicion of God, and the paranoid ideation of persecution with a hidden agenda of grandiosity.[6]

The second metaphor is that of the Holy Spirit as paraclete or helper, the one who is "'alongside' us, helping us and being an advocate for us":

> The conjunctive emotions associated with this relationship to God are intimacy, trust, communion, fellowship, and collaborative effort. When we are alienated from God, these turn into disjunctive emotions of separation, anxiety, loneliness, grief, and even depression.[7]

Taken together, these metaphors not only recognize different features of God's presence but also represent the presence of God as inherently paradoxical. On the other hand, because in Christ "the very character of God becomes incarnate 'alongside' us," the desirable shift is from being "over-against" God's presence to being "alongside."[8]

In *The Abuse of Power*, James Poling also notes the biblical tradition's representation of the dual nature of God, but rather than using the language of paradox, he refers to God's ambivalence, especially as reflected in stories concerning power struggles in which God is one of the participants. Following discussion of the tales of the rape of Tamar (2 Samuel 13), the complex story of Abraham, Sarah, Hagar, Ishmael, and Isaac (Genesis 12–22), the Flood story (Genesis 6), and Hosea 11, he concludes:

> The Hebrew Bible gives conflicting images of God for religious piety. On one hand, God is compassionate and just, protecting the vulnerable and seeking alternatives to the evil intentions of humans. But on the other hand, God is presented as insensitive to the vulnerable members of families and even destructive toward whole populations. In some ways this tension between love and hate in the image of God is unresolved.[9]

The New Testament image of God, with its emphasis on the incarnational atonement, is also problematic, and, for Poling, is not as benign as Oates's discussion of the "alongsidedness" of God implies:

> The theory of incarnational atonement seems designed to deal explicitly with the problem of the abusive God. By turning from an emphasis on wrath and sacrifice to an emphasis on suffering and imitation, God is presented as compassionate, and love is seen as more powerful than violence.
>
> However, in light of what we are learning from survivors of sexual violence, this theory also has problems. Although a benevolent parent is

> preferable to one who is abusive, the patriarchal structure of the relationship is fully intact. God is the perfect-parent who intervenes in history to save the disloyal and disobedient children. . . . The unilateral power relationship between God and humans is fully maintained. God has the power to be abusive, but God freely chooses instead to suffer in response to the evil of creation. [10]

Poling concludes that the New Testament idea of incarnational atonement has value because of its emphasis "on the search for a relational God who is fully involved in human suffering." But the issue is: "How can we discover a God of love and power who is not patriarchal and does not encourage victims to suffer?"[11] Poling believes that such an understanding of God can be found in the views of process theologian Bernard Loomer, who describes "a God of relational power whose existence includes the suffering and hope of all the creatures. . . . Everything that exists is included in God's experience."[12] In this view, "the love of God means that all the suffering of all creation is fully a part of God's experience,"[13] and "God's power is the restlessness for abundant life. It is characterized by a passion for the more—more richness, more depth and breadth, more beauty."[14] In this view, God is presented not as an ambivalent figure, but as involved in the ambiguity of all life. For Poling's own project (described in an earlier chapter), this ambiguity is reflected in the fact that "God is present in survivors' resilient hope for justice" and "God's power is present in the surprising hope of transformation in some recovering perpetrators."[15]

For Poling, this alternative understanding of God is not non-biblical; yet, for biblical connections, he turns not to the theme of Jesus' atonement, but to stories in the gospels that portray Jesus as one who provided the victims of oppression with the resources and challenges that enabled them to find power to change their lives, and who challenged the oppressors of his day to change their abusive habits and serve the God of justice.[16]

This brief summary of Poling's search for more adequate ways of speaking about God's presence, especially for those who are engaged in pastoral care and counseling, suggests that we need a way of talking about human suffering in the larger context of the suffering—the groaning and travail—of all creation. As Levertov suggests in "Urgent Whisper," the earth itself trembles "as if a beaten child or a captive animal lay waiting the next blow."[17] But it is Stafford who has the most to say about "the relational web" which is the world of God's experience.

While Poling is especially concerned with the issue of justice, however, what Stafford is especially attuned to as he hears the groaning and travailing of all creation is the cry for freedom which is so often implied in the demand for justice. What he offers us is a vision of freedom within the relational web, for freedom based on isolation and withdrawal is not real freedom. It is a denial of our interdependency, and of the fact that all members of the relational web are, at all times and in all places, deeply vulnerable.

If Poling's way of speaking of God's presence is especially reflective of the prophetic tradition of the Bible—and I believe that it is—then I would suggest that the vision Stafford sets forth in his poems is more congruent with the wisdom tradition of the Bible. This is a tradition that emphasizes the interrelated spheres of life. As Gerhard von Rad points out, one of the central wisdom texts of the Bible, the book of Proverbs, focuses on "certain basic phenomena which were observed in more or less all spheres of life," and thereby identifies the "all-embracing order" that inheres in all things.[18] Unlike those who would see no connections between the natural sphere, the human social sphere, and the inner life of the individual human self, the wisdom teachers were continually about the discernment of the common features of all spheres of life. While these spheres of life have their contradictions and puzzling aspects, they share a common order, and, because they do, analogies noted between them (for example, "Like clouds and wind without rain is a person who boasts of a gift that is not given") point to the fact that all that exists is woven together, in a great web of relationships. As von Rad notes, "One could almost say that the farther apart the subjects being compared lay, the more interesting must the discovery of analogies have been, insofar as this revealed something of the breadth of the order that was discovered."[19] Wisdom, then, is the capacity to discern the relationships between and within the various spheres of life, thus disclosing the all-embracing order of things.

If the book of Proverbs emphasizes the order that inheres in all things, it is another wisdom book, that of Job, which is especially concerned with the issue of freedom. As James Crenshaw points out, Job's demand that God be held accountable for the injustices which Job perceived in the order of things had to be set aside when it was made clear to him that the universe does not operate according to a principle of rationality but according to divine freedom. Writes Crenshaw, the "putative principle of order collapsed before divine freedom."[20]

Thus, the wisdom tradition of the Bible points to the tension that exists between our perceptions of order in the universe and the fact of divine freedom. It is not that our perceptions of order are wrong or mistaken, but we are wrong to insist that God be constrained by some principle of order, including the moral principle of order we call justice. If, with Oates and Wimberly, we are concerned about discerning the presence of God in our lives, the book of Job recommends that we look for it not where our demands for justice are met, but in moments of unexpected freedom, when the order of life is quietly relaxed, revealing the Presence of God. This, I believe, is Stafford's vision of things: He is not an anarchist, a celebrator of disorder and chaos, but a defender of a kind of relaxed order in which there is ample room for freedom. Like the shadow in the grass left by a running, leaping antelope, there are perceptible traces of God in our moments of unexpected freedom.

But let us allow Stafford to tell it in his own words, beginning with his affirmation of the universe as spirit-filled.[21]

A Spirit-Filled Universe

In Stafford's poetic world, we live in a universe that is not cold and lifeless, but alive and ultimately caring. In "What If We Were Alone?"[22] he acknowledges that the universe appears as "cold space," and yet, out there, we "glimpse company":

> What if there weren't any stars?
> What if only the sun and the earth
> circled alone in the sky? What if
> no one ever found anything outside
> this world right here?—no Galileo
> could say, "Look—it is out there,
> a hint of whether we are everything."

> Look out at the stars. Yes—cold
> space. Yes, we are so distant that
> the mind goes hollow to think it.
> But something is out there. Whatever
> our limits, we are led outward. We glimpse
> company. Each glittering point of light
> beckons: "There is something beyond."

> The moon rolls through the trees, rises
> from them, and waits. In the river all
> night a voice floats from rock

to sandbar, to log. What kind of listening
can follow quietly enough? We bow, and
the voice that falls through the rapids
calls all the rocks by their secret name.

The universe is held together—keeps company with itself—through sound. If we listen, we can hear a voice floating from here to there, ensuring that all parts sense their connectedness to the whole. The universe also beckons, invitingly, through light, which says, "There is something beyond." Light is not the end of things, but a beacon that connects us to the beyond, and leads us, confidently, outward, where we encounter more company than we ever imagined possible. The universe is not cold and empty space, but a system of intricate interrelatedness. So intimate is this interrelatedness that "the voice that falls through the rapids calls all the rocks by their secret names."

In "You Don't Know the End,"[23] Stafford suggests that the universe is spirit-filled, and, therefore, you never know what may become of a life that appears to end, but is, instead, resurrected in some other form:

Even as you are dying, a part of the world
can be your own—a badger taught me that,
with its foot in a trap on the bank of the Cimarron.

I offered the end of a stick near the lowered head:
space turned into a dream that other things had,
and four long grooves appeared on that hard wood.

My part that day was to learn. It wasn't folklore
I saw, or what anyone said, when I looked
far, past miles around me:

Wherever I went, a new life had begun,
hidden in grass, or waiting beyond the trees.
There is a spirit abiding in everything.

The learning that day was not the folk wisdom which was a part of the Cimarron country, but what a dying badger taught him about how some part of the world can always be ours. Moreover, one learns that new life is beginning everywhere one turns. Usually, it is hidden and waiting, impercep-tible to the naked eye. You and I are dying too, but what we think to be the end for us is only conjecture, for there is a spirit—new life—abiding in everything, including what is ostensibly dying.

In "By Tens"[24] Stafford reflects on "the relational web" that inheres in all things, noting the intimate connections between earth, self, and the social world:

> In my twenties the days came with a war wind
> buffeting buildings and signs. Whole forests learned
> their primitive gestures all over again and whined
> for help. Finally the storm overwhelmed mankind.
>
> In my thirties a lake of wisdom began
> its years of expansion. To promises it answered, "When?"
> And it grew by tributaries that would run
> whenever my blunders brought rebukes from anyone.
>
> In my forties a smog began to cover
> the world. At first it stayed down on the level,
> then it climbed. It sought out leaders wherever
> a leader was. It changed the world forever.
>
> In my fifties people began to move
> away from each other. Roads we traveled were of
> divergent claims. A sunset, even, would arrive
> differently on successive nights of our lives.
>
> In my sixties all that the years have brought
> begins to shine—friends, the lake of wisdom,
> the kindly curtain of smog where leaders are hidden,
> and this path of knowing that leads us all toward heaven.

Stafford uses the natural world in this poem to clarify what he has experienced in his own inner world, especially as this inner world has registered events and happenings in the social world of which he has been part. The various elements of his inner development—the primitive gestures of his twenties, the lake of wisdom in his thirties, the world-changing smog of his forties, and the altered sunsets of his fifties—have come together, in some sort of discernible order, in his sixties. What seemed most threatening then—the smog he inhaled in his forties—has taken on a more kindly demeanor, shielding him from the actions of those he would rather not know about. Also, in spite of the fact that friends have been on divergent paths, he sees us all moving on a common path—a path of knowing—that stretches its way to a heaven beyond the smog of unknowing. The images of the lake of wisdom and the path of knowing forge a link between the natural world, the inner world, and the world of human interaction. "By Tens" is a poem that not only speaks of wisdom, but also exemplifies the fundamental conviction of the biblical wisdom tradition and its perception of the order that underlies all the spheres of life, and interconnects them.

The various spheres provide a fund of similes and metaphors for illumining the other spheres, but more than this, they point to the underlying order of all things. In "Bi-Focal"[25] Stafford uses one of the spheres—the natural world—to observe that the world has another, deeper level, less ordinarily perceived, but no less real:

> Sometimes up out of this land
> a legend begins to move.
> Is it a coming near
> of something under love?
>
> Love is of the earth only,
> the surface, a map of roads
> leading wherever go miles
> or little bushes nod.
>
> Not so the legend under,
> fixed, inexorable,
> deep as the darkest mine
> the thick rocks won't tell.
>
> As fire burns the leaf
> and out of the green appears
> the vein in the center line
> and the legend veins under there,
>
> So, the world happens twice—
> once what we see it as;
> second it legends itself
> deep, the way it is.

Beneath the changing world—the surface of things—there is a foundation that is fixed, inexorable, and deep. It is deep as a mine, and as integral to the surface as the veins of a leaf.

THE VULNERABILITY OF ALL CREATION

If the world is a vast relational web, this web is fragile, and it, and the individual creatures of it, are vulnerable to exploitation. The human race is certainly the most villainous in this regard. Humankind's capacity to scorch the earth is the theme of "At the Bomb Testing Site":[26]

> At noon in the desert a panting lizard
> waited for history, its elbows tense,
> watching the curve of a particular road
> as if something might happen.
>
> It was looking at something farther off
> than people could see, an important scene
> acted in stone for little selves
> at the flute end of consequences.
>
> There was just a continent without much on it
> under a sky that never cared less.
> Ready for a change, the elbows waited.
> The hands gripped hard on the desert.

Here, the threat of human violence is registered in the larger ecosystem, as it intuitively knows that something is not right, that something fateful, and over which it has no control, is happening a few miles away.

In "Not Very Loud,"[27] the world of animals and insects keeps vigilance with the more pacific of us humans as we endure another orgy of warfare:

> Now is the time of the moths that come
> in the evening. They are around, just being
> there, at windows and doors. They crowd
> the lights, planing in from dark fields
> and liking it in town. They accept each other
> as they fly or crawl. How do they know
> what is coming? Their furred flight,
> softer than down, announces a quiet
> approach under whatever is loud.
>
> What are moths good for? Maybe they offer
> something we need, a fluttering

> near the edge of our sight, and they may carry
> whatever is needed for us to watch
> all through those long nights in our still,
> vacant houses, if there is another war.

Yet Stafford does not only point his finger at other offenders. Several of his poems concern his own violence toward the creatures of this earth. Taught by his father to hunt and fish, Stafford struggles with the fact that not all of his actions toward earth's inhabitants are simply admiring and life-respecting. In "At the Salt Marsh,"[28] he writes movingly of his empathy for the bird he has killed, and asks about the morality of what he is doing:

> Those teal with traveling wings
> had done nothing to us but they were meat
> and we waited for them with killer guns
> in the blind deceitful in the rain.
>
> They flew so arrowy till when they fell
> where the dead grass bent flat and wet
> that I looked for something after nightfall
> to come tell me why it was all right.
>
> I touched the soft head with eyes gone
> and felt through the feathers all the dark
> while we steamed our socks by the fire
> and stubborn flame licked the bark.
>
> Still I wonder, out through the raw blow
> out over the rain that levels the reeds,
> how broken parts can be wrong but true.
> I scatter my asking. I hold the duck head.

In another poem about the death of an animal, Stafford explores the meaning of what he considers a wise, if necessary, action, yet one that still disturbs him. The title, "Traveling Through the Dark,"[29] suggests that the episode has taken him through a dark pathway, where the issues are unclear and one can only hope that, in doing what he had to do, he also did what was right:

> Traveling through the dark I found a deer
> dead on the edge of the Wilson River road.

It is usually best to roll them into the canyon:
that road is narrow; to swerve might make more dead.

By glow of the tail-light I stumbled back of the car
and stood by the heap, a doe, a recent killing;
she had stiffened already, almost cold.
I dragged her off; she was large in the belly.

My fingers touching her side brought me the reason—
her side was warm; her fawn lay there waiting,
alive, still, never to be born.
Beside that mountain road I hesitated.

The car aimed ahead its lowered parking lights;
under the hood purred the steady engine.
I stood in the glare of the warm exhaust turning red;
around our group I could hear the wilderness listen.

I thought hard for us all—my only swerving—,
then pushed her over the edge into the river.

One of Stafford's most anthologized poems, "Traveling Through the Dark"
has been viewed by literary critics as a poem about the importance of making
moral judgments. It is typical, in their view, of his tendency to deliver
"injunctions, prescriptions, prohibitions, and gentle curses."[30] Yet, in explaining this poem in an interview, he noted that it "is not a poem that is
written to support a position that I have chosen, it's just a poem that grows out
of the plight I am in as a human being." He went on to say that he wanted "to
dissociate myself from taking any kind of stance that would imply that being a
writer is assuming a power of guidance or insight or anything like that." Still,
he acknowledges that his poems have been "full of issues, positions, and
attempted wisdom."[31] His phrase "attempted wisdom" is especially apropos,
as it is characteristic of the biblical wisdom tradition to deemphasize ethical
rules and moral regulations, and to affirm those judgments and decisions
which seek to restore moral order, and which are based not on what is the
right thing to do but what is the better choice among the available options.
As Walter Harrelson points out, the wisdom tradition offers a unique
alternative to the two major approaches to moral issues in ethical thinking
today. It neither attempts to "define the good for [humankind] in some total
and all-inclusive system" (philosophical ethics) nor does it "assume that the
situation itself must shape and dictate decisions" (situational ethics). Rather,

the wisdom tradition would give us examples of various kinds of conduct and let us learn what we can from such examples. It would give these to us in sharp pictures, deeply etched into the consciousness, taught to us when young, not sprung on us only as needed. [32]

Stafford's conduct in "Traveling Through the Dark"—his thinking hard for us all—is such an example, and that kind of picture.

Stafford is aware that violence and treachery are not limited to human-kind, that they occur among the other species as well. When they happen, as in "Chickens the Weasel Killed," [33] humans are often unable to intervene, but can only stand by, feeling the vulnerability of the victim:

> A passerby being fair about sacrifice,
> with no program but walking,
> no acrobat of salvation,
> I couldn't help seeing the weasel
> fasten on the throat.
>
> Any vision isolates:
> those chickens the weasel killed—
> I hear them relax years from now,
> subsiding while they threaten,
> and then appeal to the ground with their wings.

A vulnerability inheres in all of life, and no one of us—no living creature—is safe and secure. Our solidarity with other creatures is not in our power and strength, but in our vulnerability, as in this sense, we are just like them.

In "Behind the Falls" [34] he addresses our own experiences of fear and dread which reveal our vulnerability:

> First the falls, then the cave:
> then sheets of sound around us fell
> while earth fled inward, where we went.
> We traced it back, cigarette lighter high—
> lost the roof, then the wall,
> found abruptly in that space
> only the flame and ourselves,
> and heard the curtain like the earth

go down, so still it made the lighter
dim that led us on under the hill.

We stopped, afraid—lost
if ever that flame went out—
and surfaced in each other's eyes,
two real people suddenly
more immediate in the dark
than in the sun we'd ever be.
When men and women meet that way
the curtain of the earth descends, and they
find how faint the light has been, how far
mere honesty or justice is from all they need.

In such immediacy, the darkness closing in upon us, and frightened out of
our minds, honesty and justice are not what we need. We need light to show
us the way of escape. Yet precisely because we are vulnerable, we are more
immediate to one another.

HOLDING THE EARTH IN OUR PRAYERS

Given our common vulnerability, Stafford suggests that we need to hold
the whole fragile earth in our prayers. What is needed is not more laws, or
more fences, but a deeper involvement in the spirit that inheres in all things.
In his poem "Watching the Jet Planes Dive,"[35] he suggests that the
appropriate response to the threat overhead is to go back to customs and
rituals we have left behind:

We must go back and find a trail on the ground
back of the forest and mountain on the slow land;
we must begin to circle on the intricate sod.
By such wild beginnings without help we may find
the small trail on through the buffalo-bean vines.

We must go back with noses and the palms of our hands,
and climb over the map in far places, everywhere,
and lie down whenever there is doubt and sleep there.
If roads are unconnected we must make a path,
no matter how far it is, or how lowly we arrive.

We must find something forgotten by everyone alive,
and make some fabulous gesture when the sun goes down
as they do by custom in little Mexico towns
where they crawl for some ritual up a rocky steep.
The jet planes dive; we must travel on our knees.

In "Like a Little Stone,"[36] he makes an even more direct appeal for prayers in behalf of the great earth:

Like a little stone, feel the shadow of the great earth;
let distance pierce you till you cling to trees.
That the world may be all the same,
close your eyes till everything is,
    and the farthest sand can vote.

Making the world be big by hunting its opposite,
go out gleaning for lost lions
that are terrified by valleys of still lambs,
for hummingbirds that dream before each wingbeat,
    for the mole that met the sun.

If time won't let a thing happen, hurry there,
to the little end of the cone that darkness bends.
Any place where you turn but might have gone on,
all possibilities need you there.
    The centers of stones need your prayers.

If we are to befriend the earth, to hold it in our prayers, this is because it has already befriended us, and because its common splendors are cause for our rejoicing. Such is the affirmation of "Earth Dweller":[37]

It was all the clods at once become
precious; it was the barn, and the shed,
and the windmill, my hands, the crack
Arlie made in the axe handle: oh, let me stay
here humbly, forgotten, to rejoice in it all;
let the sun casually rise and set.
If I have not found the right place,
teach me; for, somewhere inside, the clods are

vaulted mansions, lines through the barn sing
for the saints forever, the shed and windmill
rear so glorious the sun shudders like a gong.

Now I know why people worship, carry around
magic emblems, wake up talking dreams
they teach to their children: the world speaks.
The world speaks everything to us.
It is our only friend.

We are also to pray for one another. In one of his most beautiful poems, "Vespers,"[38] Stafford explores the thought that a poem may "arrange a kind of prayer" for another:

As the living pass, they bow
till they imitate stones.
In the steep mountains then
those millions remind us:
    every fist the wind has
    loses against those faces.

And at the end of the day
when every rock on the west
claims a fragment of sun,
a last bird comes, wing and
    then wing over the valley
    and over the valley, and home,

Till unbound by our past we sing
wherever we go, ready or not,
stillness above and below, the slowed
evening carried in prayer toward the end.
    You know who you are:
    This is for you, my friend.

"Vespers" has the tone of an evening prayer: reflective, meditative, quiet, peaceful. It reverences those who have passed on; it takes note of the last bird who at the end of day comes winging home; and it quietly celebrates the freedom we have come to experience from our past. On another day, such freedom might be expressed in brave and confident talk, but tonight, what prevails is a spirit of peace and repose, a sense of the "stillness above and below," of the "slowed evening" being carried in prayer toward the day's end. At times like this, we reach out and assure the other, "You know who you are: This is for you, my friend." "Vespers" is a gift, a gift of thoughtfulness, offering the assurance that only friends can offer each other: the assurance that the other will always be held in prayer.

THE PRESENCE OF GOD

By emphasizing that the world is spirit-filled, Stafford would appear to be advocating a kind of nature mysticism, and some of his interpreters have called him a mystic. Critic Gerald Burns suggests that Stafford stands "in the American pattern of mysticism, a heritage from Edwards, Emerson, and Whitman, preaching wonder and calling us to recognize the physical world around us."[39] But Stafford once told an interviewer that he does not feel mystical, that he only feels "driven into uttering things that must seem quite tame to other people."[40] Perhaps Stephen Grey's suggestion that Stafford has a "dogged faith in the teaching power of Nature" is therefore closer to the mark.[41]

His image of God is a reflection of the priority he gives to the teaching power of Nature, for virtually all of his poems that have reference to God are situated in the world of nature. In "At the Summit"[42] he tells of traveling from the plains to the mountains, eventually arriving at the Great Divide. The drive westward took him through wheatfields "Turning in God's hand green to pale to yellow, like the season gradual—." In "Along Highway 40"[43] he is again on the open road, traveling much slower than those "martyrs" who were heading toward Nevada and the gaming tables. He let "the speedometer measure God's kindness, and slept in the wilderness on the hard ground." In "A Glimpse in the Crowd,"[44] God slows the parachute that has been falling for years: "He can't stop it, but he can let you look back," taking stock, before "you begin falling again." In "A Walk in the Country"[45] he tells of being out walking alone late one night when a terrible thing happened:

> the world, wide, unbearably bright,
> had leaped on me. I carried mountains.
> Though there was much I knew, though
> kind people turned away,
> I walked there ashamed—

> into that still picture
> to bring my fear and pain.
>
> By dawn I felt all right;
> my hair was covered with dew;
> the light was bearable; the air
> came still and cool.
> And God had come back there
> to carry the world again.

We are not told the nature of this terrible shaming experience. All we know is that, for a time, he carried a crushing burden—fear and pain—and that, in the morning, God had come back to carry the world again.

In these poems, God is a presence with human features, legs to walk with, hands to turn the wheat with, hands to restrain us from falling, and a back to carry the world. These images of God's own body portray God as a presence who acts in human lives, but does so quietly and imperceptibly, not with fanfare, force, or the perception of heavy exertion. In "Walking West"[46] God is again portrayed as having legs to walk with, but here what most impresses itself on the human walker is God's habit of stopping still, listening to the almost imperceptible sounds of nature:

> Anyone with quiet pace who
> walks a gray road in the West
> may hear a badger underground where
> in deep flint another time is
>
> Caught by flint and held forever,
> the quiet pace of God stopped still.
> Anyone who listens walks on
> time that dogs him single file,
>
> To mountains that are far from people,
> the face of the land gone gray like flint.
> Badgers dig their little lives there,
> quiet-paced the land lies gaunt,
>
> The railroad dies by a yellow depot,
> town falls away toward a muddy creek.
> Badger-gray the sod goes under
> a river of wind, a hawk on a stick.

Hearing something occurring underground, God stops still, and the event takes on a still-life quality, drawn out, and "held forever." We might say, then, that any reference to God in a poem by Stafford places the event or experience being described or recounted in the context of eternity. By alluding to God in the poem, he says that a particular life experience, however insignificant or ordinary it may seem, belongs, in some special way, to our primordial past and our unchartable future. For reasons we cannot fathom, some experiences are like this. They hold forever.

If God favors stillness, though, God is also capable of lashing out in anger. In "The Tillamook Burn"[47] Stafford focuses on God's involvement in a massive forest fire:

> These mountains have heard God;
> they burned for weeks. He spoke
> in a tongue of flame from sawmill trash
> and you can read His word down to the rock.
>
> In milky rivers the steelhead
> butt upstream to spawn
> and find a world with depth again,
> starting from stillness and water across gray stone.
>
> Inland along the canyons
> all night weather smokes
> past the deer and the widow-makers—
> trees too dead to fell till again He speaks,
>
> Mowing the criss-cross trees and the listening peaks.

Here is the angry side of God, whose tongue of flame was spoken from sawmill trash. This is surely poetic—and divine—justice, for if one lives by the saw, one must be prepared to die from the burning. Then, as though to underscore that God's first speech-act was no accident, God speaks again, using fiery wind to level the dead trees. Where, in earlier poems, we encountered the feet, the hands, the back of God, we now feel the heat of God's voice, and it is terrible.

If a number of Stafford's poems reflect the sense we have of God's presence, one, at least, is concerned with God's inaccessibility. In the poem "Ultimate Problems,"[48] he addresses the fact that we humans have different ways of understanding why God seems so far away, which arises out of our unique experiences of life in the world:

In the Aztec design God crowds
into the little pea that is rolling
out of the picture.
All the rest extends bleaker
because God has gone away.

In the White Man design, though,
no pea is there.
God is everywhere,
but hard to see.
The Aztecs frown at this.

How do you know He is everywhere?
And how did He get out of the pea?

Both cultures have experience of being bereft of God, the one finding God hard to see, the other sensing that God leaves them from time to time, rolling right out of the picture. Yet, is God's absence due to God's omnipresence, making God seem everywhere but nowhere in particular? Or is God's absence due to God being crowded into one very small part of the world—the smallest imaginable—and imprisoned there? In the one view, God is dispersed, the divine reflection of westward expansion. In the other, God is highly localized, the personification of restricted movement and spatial concentration. These are two very different ways of visualizing God's place in the total relational web of life, and Stafford makes no attempt to choose between them. Yet, his sympathies lie with the Aztecs, as he wants to affirm with them that, while God is surely universal, God is also local, concentrated in life's ordinary places and things.

JESUS, THE WANDERER

If Stafford's God is linked to the world of nature, so too is his image of Jesus. For him, Jesus is a stranger whose influence is felt precisely because he will not be contained by local history, captive to local stories and ways, but, instead, is a wanderer, like Stafford himself, drawing others out from all this, to the hills, even to the edge of continents. In "What God Used for Eyes Before We Came,"[49] he comments on the way that Jesus came, "irresistible, calm over irrelevant history toward a continent wall that moth rays touch." In "Sunset: Southwest,"[50] he envisions Jesus, on the day the world ends, looking far into the distance:

In front of the courthouse holding the adaptable flag
Jesus will be here the day the world ends
looking off there into the sky-bore
past Socorro over sunset lands.

There will be torque in all the little towns,
wind will beat upon the still
face of anyone, just anyone,
who will stand and turn the still

Face to full dial staring out there
and then the world will be all—
the face hearing only the world
bloom from the eyes, and fall.

Since Jesus' eyes are drawn to places far beyond our towns and cities, toward "the sky-bore past Socorro over sunset lands," he is associated in Stafford's poems with far places, and the edges of things. He does not belong anywhere, and, judging from his relatively few appearances in Stafford's poems, he does not assume a controlling role in the poet's own story. Yet, he is significant precisely because he is so much like the poet himself: a wanderer, a visionary, a man whose spirit will not be controlled by local allegiances and local ways of making and keeping time. His eyes are on the wind and sky, and seem to say: Do not look me full in the face, but attend to where I am looking. Do not make me the object of your attention, but take upon yourselves the lighter burden of looking out where I have looked. Follow my eyes.

DEGREES OF FREEDOM

Stafford's images of God and of Jesus are not images of control. They are images of the beyond, of the eternal, of that which survives and lasts. This is altogether consistent with his view that what vulnerable individuals need most is not that justice will be served, but that they will experience some degrees of freedom. In "In Camp,"[51] a reflection on his experience as a conscientious objector during World War II, he describes his sense of being a prisoner, one who yearned not for justice but to be free:

That winter of the war, every day
sprang outward. I was a prisoner.
Someone brought me gifts. That year

now is far: birds can't fly
the miles to find a forgotten cause.

No task I do today has justice
at the end. All I know is
my degree of leaning in this wind
where—once the mind springs free—
every cause has reason
but reason has no law.

In camps like that, if I should go again,
I'd still study the gospel and play the accordion.

What seems to concern him about laws designed to legislate justice is that they undermine the human spirit, which is already too willing to relinquish itself to systems of thought and governance. For him, the challenge is getting and staying free when everything around us conspires to restrict our movement and to deplete and suffocate our souls. Also, in retrospect, he can no longer recall the just cause for which he struggled, but he can surely remember studying the gospel and playing the accordion, and he would do this again, as they represented freedom.

On the other hand, the cry for freedom may itself become a mere slogan that only enslaves. As "The Dean at Faculty Retreat"[52] suggests, the Dean knows and exploits this fact:

They go by, dragging their chains. I hook
to each a little rubber band and slip
the tether to a stake at the end. They go on
but after a time their heads turn. They
stop. Slowly I walk toward them
talking quietly and calling their names.
On their necks I hang their slogan, any color
they like: "Freedom," fastened to the chain.

Or we can retreat from freedom because we would rather cling to our own notions of how to get free than avail ourselves of the chances for freedom that already exist. Here is an excerpt from "A Message from the Wanderer":[53]

Today outside your prison I stand
and rattle my walking stick: Prisoners, listen;

you have relatives outside. And there are
thousands of ways to escape.

Years ago I bent my skill to keep my
cell locked, had chains smuggled to me in pies,
and shouted my plans to jailers;
but always new plans occurred to me,
or the new heavy locks bent hinges off,
or some stupid jailer would forget
and leave the keys.

. . . .

Thus freedom always came nibbling my thought,
just as—often, in light, on the open hills—
you can pass an antelope and not know
and look back, and then—even before you see—
there is something wrong about the grass.
And then you see.

Freedom typically takes us by surprise, and is not something we may
carefully orchestrate. It comes to us, and then, in retrospect, we see it for
what it is, as imperceptible but as real as the form the grass takes when an
antelope has run through. Freedom, then, is the other side of the fact of our
vulnerability. We have grounds for fear, and there are many ways that we can
become entrapped, ensnared, and eventually destroyed. Our vulnerability is
ever with us. Yet, as he claims in "Freedom,"[54] we are also never without a
certain margin of freedom:

> Freedom is not following a river.
> Freedom is following a river,
>   though, if you want to.
> It is deciding now by what happens now.
> It is knowing that luck makes a difference.
>
> No leader is free; no follower is free—
>   the rest of us can often be free.
> Most of the world are living by
> creeds too odd, chancy, and habit-forming
>   to be worth arguing about by reason.

If you are oppressed, wake up about
four in the morning: most places,
you can usually be free some of the time
if you wake up before other people.

There are choices we can make, little things we can do or avoid, which allow us to be free. Creeds are not a good idea as they are addictive and not conducive to freedom. Luck is a good thing to keep in mind, as it sometimes makes the difference between oppression and freedom. Choosing for now, and not in light of times past or future, also helps. Being up and about when what oppresses us is taking its rest is also a good idea. There are no set formulas for freedom, but we do have choices. We are not without some freedom to choose what we will or will not do.

If there are no set formulas for freedom, there is a kind of wisdom that is conducive to freedom. In "The Little Ways That Encourage Good Fortune,"[55] Stafford identifies this type of wisdom:

Wisdom is having things right in your life
and knowing why.
If you do not have things right in your life
you will be overwhelmed:
you may be heroic, but you will not be wise.
If you have things right in your life
but do not know why,
you are just lucky, and you will not move
in the little ways that encourage good fortune.

The saddest are those not right in their lives
who are acting to make things right for others:
they act only from the self—
and that self will never be right:
no luck, no help, no wisdom.

The wisdom that enhances our prospects for freedom involves knowing what we need to do to avoid being overwhelmed in life. This usually means keeping life simple and uncomplicated, and not inviting unnecessary trouble. It means having things right in your own life before you go about trying to set the lives of others right. (Recall his poem about his sister, who "went out into the world to right its wrongs.")

In "Outside"[56] Stafford observes that the more we try to contain or control what threatens us, restricting its own freedom to act, the more it threatens and controls us:

> The least little sound sets the coyotes walking,
> walking the edge of our comfortable earth.
> We look inward, but all of them
> are looking toward us as they walk the earth.
>
> We need to let animals loose in our houses,
> the wolf to escape with a pan in his teeth,
> and streams of animals toward the horizon
> racing with something silent in each mouth.
>
> For all we have taken into our keeping
> and polished with our hands belongs to a truth
> greater than ours, in the animals' keeping.
> Coyotes are circling around our truth.

We enforce our rules, hoping to make the world more secure and more civilized, yet, in so doing, we only violate a deeper truth, and find ourselves more besieged than ever. If you wish to neutralize those who threaten you, do not try to keep them out, but let them roam freely in your house, where their actions against you are clearly visible.

Another way to know freedom is to give our attention to "real things" and leave aside the dreams which are created out of dread, wonder, and the desire to be heroic. In "Allegiances,"[57] Stafford suggests that we cling instead to life's common things:

> It is time for all the heroes to go home
> if they have any, time for all of us common ones
> to locate ourselves by the real things
> we live by.
>
> Far to the north, or indeed in any direction,
> strange mountains and creatures have always lurked—
> elves, goblins, trolls, and spiders:—we
> encounter them in dread and wonder,
>
> But once we have tasted far streams, touched the gold,
> found some limit beyond the waterfall,

a season changes, and we come back, changed
but safe, quiet, grateful.

Suppose an insane wind holds all the hills
while strange beliefs whine at the traveler's ears,
we ordinary beings can cling to the earth and love
where we are, sturdy for common things.

Stafford's appeal to a kind of quietism may imply that he opposes activism, believing that freedom comes from non-involvement. Yet, in a poem entitled "Monuments for a Friendly Girl at a Tenth Grade Party,"[58] he celebrates the life of a young woman who was an activist, but on her own terms:

The only relics left are those long
spangled seconds our school clock chipped out
when you crossed the social hall
and we found each other alive,
by our glances never to accept our town's
ways, torture for advancement,
nor ever again be prisoners by choice.

Now I learn you died
serving among the natives of Garden City,
Kansas, part of a Peace Corps
before governments thought of it.

Ruth, over the horizon your friends eat
foreign chaff and have addresses like titles,
but for you the crows and hawks patrol
the old river. May they never
forsake you, nor you need monuments
other than this I make, and the one
I hear clocks chip in that world we found.

In Ruth, he found someone who shared his own desire to break out of his town's ways, and his determination not to be a prisoner by choice. She lived out that freedom, and his prayer is that the crows and hawks that patrol the river for her will never forsake her. She was an activist, but more to the point, she was a free woman. As his poem "Freedom" says, "Freedom is not following a river. Freedom is following a river, though, if you want to." She followed her river, and now the crows and hawks keep vigilance over it and her.

HEARING THE SILENT CRIES FOR RELEASE

In recent years, a number of books by pastoral theologians have talked about pastoral care in the context of liberation. Edward and Anne Wimberly have used the theme of liberation to write about pastoral care among African American Christians.[59] James E. Dittes has written eloquently about liberation for men and for women.[60] In emphasizing freedom, Stafford's poetry exhibits a similar concern, and is the poet's gift to those of us who have long believed that the fundamental purpose of pastoral care is to help others gain a new margin of freedom. Such freedom need not be at the expense of connectedness, or "the relational web" of which James Poling speaks. Rather, freedom is what enables us to experience life as a web, not a tether, much less a chain. And pastoral care involves the capacity to hear—to listen for—the other's cry for release from one or more prisons of human devising.

If we have learned anything over the past several decades about what makes real pastoral care possible, it is that pastoral care involves the capacity to listen. Howard Clinebell prefaces his chapter on "The Foundation of All Types of Caring and Counseling" with this quotation from Dietrich Bonhoeffer:

> Many people are looking for an ear that will listen. They do not find it among Christians, because Christians are talking when they should be listening. He who no longer listens to his brother [or sister] will soon no longer be listening to God either. . . . One who cannot listen long and patiently will presently be talking beside the point and never really speaking to others, albeit he be not conscious of it.[61]

It is often said that humans differ from all the other species in their capacity to speak, to use language, and certainly poetry itself testifies to this unique human capacity. But Stafford uses his gift of language in a subversive way, to stress and to celebrate the human capacity, which we share with other species, to listen, to be attentive to the sounds around, above, and beneath us. Affirmation of our capacity to speak can become a kind of human triumphalism, an assertion of our superiority to the other creatures on the face of this earth. Recognition of our capacity for listening is a form of modesty, for here, we are more often than not inferior to the other species, as they tend to hear more acutely and with greater sensitivity to the meaning, significance, and consequences of sounds. A persistent theme in Stafford's poetry is the role played by birds, animals, trees, and even stones in listening for us, and the conviction that we, in turn, derive insights into what the world is trying to be by listening to other creatures, as they hear at a much deeper level than we.

Also, while we, in pastoral care, give particular attention to listening to other human selves, to hearing human sighs too deep for words, Stafford is saying that we also need to listen for the sounds that the world itself is making, and thus to hear human cries and sighs as part of the deep intentionality of the world. Conversely, we come to know what the world is trying to be by hearing the particular and peculiar cries of one of its inhabitants, for we come to know the world through immersion in the local, and not by some general mapping of the whole. This is the lesson his father taught him in "Listening," a poem introduced in chapter 1.[62]

> My father could hear a little animal step,
> or a moth in the dark against the screen,
> and every far sound called the listening out
> into places where the rest of us had never been.
>
> More spoke to him from the soft wild night
> than came to our porch for us on the wind;
> we would watch him look up and his face go keen
> till the walls of the world flared, widened.
>
> My father heard so much that we still stand
> inviting the quiet by turning the face,
> waiting for a time when something in the night
> will touch us too from that other place.

Fortunately, those of us who have made pastoral care our special vocation in life are already disposed to privilege the local, the specific, the particular, the one and only. But what we have not emphasized sufficiently is the connectedness between the deep needs of the individual and the earth's correspondingly deep desire to be what it is trying to be. Only a few of us, those who are saying that pastoral care needs to be grounded in earth care, in an appreciation for the ecosystem, have pressed this point.[63] In his sermon, "The Care of the Earth," Joseph Sittler quotes extensively from the poet

Richard Wilbur, noting that the poet affirms the simple and absolute point that our "selfhood hangs upon the persistence of the earth," while earth's "dear known and remembered factualness is the matrix of the self."[64]

Stafford's poetry is rooted in his sense of the connectedness of all things, a conviction which he shares with the wisdom tradition of the Bible. This conviction is not based solely on the notion that some phenomena in the world invite analogies with other phenomena (e.g., the "storm" within my "soul"), but on the more fundamental conviction that, within the world, there is a deep structure—a veining—which links everything to everything else. By noting the connectedness that runs through all things—this relational web—Stafford can affirm the convergence of the needs of the individual and the desire of the earth to be what it is trying to be.

If Stafford is right, the cry we hear most persistently, whatever the specific problem may be, is the silent, plaintive, or anguished cry for freedom. For him, there are too many unnecessary fences and false and arbitrary restrictions on our movements on the earth. There is also too much possessiveness and acquisitiveness, the hoarding of goods that belong to the earth. There is too much concern about security, resulting in the creation of fortresses designed to keep our enemies out, while they only succeed in keeping us imprisoned inside.

Freedom, of course, can be deceptive, and what seems to be freeing may not be so. While physical distance and emotional withdrawal may help it to happen, freedom is not synonymous with isolation, for freedom comes with recognizing and accepting the interconnectedness of all things. Yet, freedom means knowing that our connectedness is not sustained by roping us off or chaining us together, but by subtle threads that enable us to keep in touch with one another. In "Connections,"[65] Stafford notes that the thread which holds us together is beyond touch and sight, but this doesn't mean it isn't there:

> Ours is a low, curst, under-swamp land
> the raccoon puts his hand in,
> gazing through his mask for tendrils
> that will hold it all together.
>
> No touch can find that thread, it is too small.
> Sometimes we think we learn its course—
> through evidence no court allows
> a sneeze may glimpse us Paradise.

> But ways without a surface we can find
> flash through the mask only by surprise—
> a touch of mud, a raccoon smile.
>
> And if we purify the pond, the lilies die.

We know that a thread runs through all of life when achieving something here has a harmful effect over there. Nothing is an island unto itself, and freedom is not a matter of cutting the thread that binds us together, but of holding the thread lightly, letting it tighten and loosen as it will. Freedom also comes with knowing that the thread, like telegraph lines on the midwestern plains, reaches all the way to Paradise. To know that there is a reality far, far beyond us, yet lightly linked to ours, is to know that there is always the possibility of freedom. This is not the freedom that comes merely with leaving home or town, though sometimes this helps, but a freedom far deeper and infinitely more real, one that comes with knowing that we live in a bi-focal world that always happens twice: once as we see it, and once as it legends itself deep, the way it is.

If hearing and responding to cries for freedom is what pastoral care is essentially about, we need to be vigilant—careful—that we do not, through well-meant efforts to help, find ourselves holding the threads too tightly, like a puppeteer. Knowing there is always the danger of indifference, neglect, and our own fatigue, we may insist on taking control of another's life precisely where that person is struggling to experience freedom. Or we affirm the fact that freedom is what they want and need, but we insist that they find it our way. Like the faculty dean, we help them put a freedom sign around their necks, and the symbol takes the place of genuine freedom. To this temptation to control or insist on our own prescription for deliverance, Stafford's poem, "There Is Blindness,"[66] is a valuable antidote:

> There is blindness; there is
> vision: accepting the symptoms
> is not helping the victim.
>
> Brought close and loud, faces
> remind you—you deserve anger,
> even their anger:
>
> Pain is real.

But over their shoulders
there looms real home—

There's the world.

Pastors who want others to know freedom need to be free enough themselves
to allow others to turn and greet the world that the pastor can neither be nor
represent, to see not as the pastor sees, but to follow the eyes of Jesus.

On the other hand, pastors might do more than they are doing at present to
teach and encourage others to live wisely, for wisdom is so often the key to
finding freedom. Pastors might take greater advantage of opportunities to talk
about the "little ways that encourage good fortune."[67] Pastors have expertise
in these matters growing out of their experiences with many individuals who
have not known how to live wisely, and with many other individuals who are
exemplars of wisdom. Often, the reason why some persons are in the former
group and others in the latter is itself small and seemingly insignificant,
owing, for example, to the fact that one person was given useful advice by a
parent, a teacher, or an older sibling, while the other was not.

Pastors have been reluctant to speak about "the little ways that encourage
good fortune" because "good fortune" has been understood in our time and place
as material success. But the good fortune of which Stafford speaks is the living of
satisfying daily lives, where our spirits are free and there is joy in our hearts. Such
good fortune is not about material success, possessions, or self-promotion at the
expense of others, but about having things right in our lives and knowing why.

There is no set formula for getting things right, no approach or method that
will work for all of us all of the time. Yet Stafford's observation that if you get up
at four in the morning, your chances of knowing some freedom are good,
suggests that freedom often comes from making small adjustments. Increasingly,
psychotherapists are also suggesting that real change is often achieved through
small modifications in the ways we conduct our daily lives, challenging the
commonsense assumption that the amount of change is directly proportionate to
the amount of force exerted to effect the change.[68] As Stafford puts it:

Freedom is not following a river.
Freedom is following a river,
though, if you want to.

And God is the one who underwrites our freedom to choose.

174

NOTES

INTRODUCTION

1. See, for example, Charles V. Gerkin, *The Living Human Document* (Nashville: Abingdon Press, 1984); and Eugene H. Peterson, *Five Smooth Stones for Pastoral Work* (Atlanta: John Knox Press, 1980), especially ch. 2, "The Pastoral Work of Story-Making: Ruth."

2. See John Dominic Crossan, *In Parables: The Challenge of the Historical Jesus* (New York: Harper & Row, 1973); idem, *The Dark Interval: Towards a Theology of Story* (Niles, Ill.: Argus Communications, 1975).

3. See Donald Capps, *Biblical Approaches to Pastoral Counseling* (Philadelphia: Westminster Press, 1981), ch. 4; idem, *Pastoral Care and Hermeneutics* (Philadelphia: Fortress Press, 1984), ch. 5; idem, *Reframing: A New Method in Pastoral Care* (Minneapolis: Fortress Press, 1990), chs. 3–5.

4. See Capps, *Pastoral Care and Hermeneutics*, ch. 2.

5. Ibid.

6. Charles V. Gerkin, *Widening the Horizons: Pastoral Responses to a Fragmented Society* (Philadelphia: Westminster Press, 1986).

CHAPTER 1

1. Gary L. Harbaugh, *The Pastor as Person: Maintaining Personal Integrity in the Choices and Challenges of Ministry* (Minneapolis: Augsburg, 1984), p. 9.

2. Denise Levertov, *New and Selected Essays* (New York: New Directions Books, 1992), p. 4.

3. Harbaugh, *The Pastor as Person*, p. 147. See also "The Minister's Self-Knowledge," ch. 5 of Daniel Day Williams's *The Minister and the Care of Souls* (New York: Harper & Row, 1961), pp. 95–121.

4. William Stafford, *Passwords* (New York: HarperCollins, 1991), p. xiii.

5. William Stafford, *Stories That Could Be True: New and Collected Poems* (New York: Harper & Row, 1977), p. 67.

6. Ibid., p. 66.

7. Ibid., p. 98.

8. William Stafford, *A Glass Face in the Rain: New Poems* (New York: Harper & Row, 1982), p. 84.

9. Stafford, *Stories That Could Be True*, p. 180.

10. Stafford, *A Glass Face in the Rain*, p. 75.

11. William Stafford, *An Oregon Message* (New York: Harper & Row, 1987), p. 103.

12. Ibid., p. 93.

13. Stafford, *Stories That Could Be True*, p. 246.

14. Stafford, *An Oregon Message*, p. 105.

15. Stafford, *Stories That Could Be True*, pp. 111–112.

16. Stafford, *An Oregon Message*, p. 95.

17. Stafford, *A Glass Face in the Rain*, p. 69.

18. Stafford, *An Oregon Message*, p. 15.

19. Ibid., p. 30.

20. Stafford, *Stories That Could Be True*, p. 33.

21. Ibid., pp. 62–63.

22. Stafford, *Passwords*, p. 20.

23. Stafford, *Stories That Could Be True*, p. 107.

24. Ibid., p. 29.

25. Ibid., p. 185.

26. Ibid., p. 231.

27. Stafford, *A Glass Face in the Rain*, p. 91.

28. Stafford, *An Oregon Message*, p. 97.

29. Stafford, *Stories That Could Be True*, p. 156.

30. Stafford, *A Glass Face in the Rain*, p. 72.

31. Stafford, *Stories That Could Be True*, pp. 120–121.

32. Ibid., p. 114.

33. Stafford, *A Glass Face in the Rain*, p. 13.

34. Stafford, *Stories That Could Be True*, p. 64.

35. Ibid., pp. 83–84.

36. Ibid., pp. 161–162.

37. Stafford, *A Glass Face in the Rain*, p. 106.

38. Ibid., p. 37.

39. Stafford, *Stories That Could Be True*, pp. 118–119.

40. Stafford, *An Oregon Message*, p. 91.

41. Ibid., p. 35.

42. Stafford, *Stories That Could Be True*, p. 113.

43. Ibid., p. 220.

44. Ibid., p. 107.

45. Ibid., pp. 9–10.

46. Ibid., p. 115.

47. See Deborah A. Straub, ed., *Contemporary Authors*, New Revision Series, vol. 22 (Detroit: Gale Research, 1988), p. 440.

48. Gaylord Noyce, *The Minister as Moral Counselor* (Nashville: Abingdon Press, 1989), p. 16.

49. Donald Capps, *Life Cycle Theory and Pastoral Care* (Philadelphia: Fortress Press, 1983), ch. 5; idem, *Pastoral Care and Hermeneutics* (Philadelphia: Fortress Press, 1984), chs. 3–5; idem, *Reframing: A New Method in Pastoral Care* (Minneapolis: Fortress Press, 1990), ch. 8. See Alastair V. Campbell, *Rediscovering Pastoral Care* (Philadelphia: Westminster Press, 1981).

50. Stafford, *Stories That Could Be True*, p. 52.

CHAPTER 2

1. Gaylord Noyce, *The Art of Pastoral Conversation* (Atlanta: John Knox Press, 1981), p. 3.

2. Ibid., p. 7.

3. Ibid., pp. 9–10.

4. Ibid., p. 46.

5. Ibid., pp. 49–50.

6. Carl R. Rogers, *On Becoming a Person* (Boston: Houghton Mifflin, 1961), p. 284.

7. Carl R. Rogers, *Client-Centered Therapy* (Boston: Houghton Mifflin, 1951), p. 29.

8. Ibid., pp. 110–111.

9. Rogers, *On Becoming a Person*, pp. 147–148.

10. Ibid., p. 148.

11. Ibid., pp. 148–149.

12. Ibid., p. 113.

13. Ibid.

14. Ibid., p. 189.

15. See Donald Capps, *Pastoral Care: A Thematic Approach* (Philadelphia: Westminster Press, 1979), ch. 3; idem, *Pastoral Counseling and Preaching* (Philadelphia: Westminster Press, 1980), ch. 2; idem, *Reframing*, ch. 1. I am not suggesting,

however, that key features of the client-centered approach, such as empathic understanding, are inappropriate for problem-solving pastoral counseling. My point is simply that, in the parish context, it is necessary for counseling to be more specific from the outset as to anticipated goals and the time frame within which such goals will be accomplished.

16. Denise Levertov, *Collected Earlier Poems 1940–1960* (New York: New Directions Books, 1979), pp. 77–78.

17. See Donald J. Greiner, ed., *Dictionary of Literary Biography*, vol. 5, pt. 2 (Detroit: Gale Research, 1980), p. 4.

18. Levertov, *Collected Earlier Poems 1940–1960*, p. 10.

19. Greiner, ed., *Dictionary of Literary Biography*, p. 5.

20. Ibid., p. 7.

21. See Tracy Chevalier, ed., *Contemporary Poets* (Chicago: St. James Press, 1991), p. 555.

22. Denise Levertov, *Poems 1968–1972* (New York: New Directions Books, 1987), pp. 12–13.

23. Denise Levertov, *Poems 1960–1967* (New York: New Directions Books, 1983), pp. 120–121.

24. Ibid., p. 70.

25. Denise Levertov, *Candles in Babylon* (New York: New Directions Books, 1982), p. 6.

26. Denise Levertov, *Life in the Forest* (New York: New Directions Books, 1978), pp. 122–123.

27. Denise Levertov, *Oblique Prayers* (New York: New Directions Books, 1984), p. 17.

28. Ibid., p. 31.

29. Denise Levertov, *Breathing the Water* (New York: New Directions Books, 1988), p. 45.

30. Levertov, *Life in the Forest*, p. 93.

31. Levertov, *Poems 1968–1972*, p. 18.

32. Ibid., p. 232.

33. Denise Levertov, *Evening Train* (New York: New Directions Books, 1992), p. 32.

34. Ibid., p. 29.

35. Denise Levertov, *A Door in the Hive* (New York: New Directions Books, 1989), p. 90.

36. Levertov, *Collected Earlier Poems 1940–1960*, p. 11.

37. Levertov, *Poems 1968–1972*, p. 64.

38. Noyce, *The Art of Pastoral Conversation*, p. 10.

39. Levertov, *Poems 1960–1967,* p. 92.

40. Eugene T. Gendlin, *Focusing,* 2d ed. (New York: Bantam Books, 1981), p. 69.

41. James E. Dittes, "The Mitigated Self," in Richard K. Fenn and Donald Capps, eds., *the Endangered Self* (Princeton, N.J., The Center for Religion, Self and Society of Princeton Theological Seminary, 1992), p. 82.

42. Levertov, *Poems 1968–1972,* p. 246.

43. Levertov, *Life in the Forest,* p. 39.

44. Levertov, *Poems 1960–1967,* p. 170.

CHAPTER 3

1. Kenneth R. Mitchell and Herbert Anderson, *All Our Losses, All Our Griefs: Resources for Pastoral Care* (Philadelphia: Westminster Press, 1983), p. 15.

2. Ibid., pp. 36–46.

3. Ibid., pp. 46–51.

4. Ibid., pp. 88–89.

5. Ibid., p. 88.

6. Ibid., p. 126.

7. Sigmund Freud, "Mourning and Melancholia," in James Strachey, ed., *Standard Edition of the Complete Psychological Works of Sigmund Freud,* vol. 14 (London: Hogarth Press, 1957), pp. 152–170.

8. Mitchell and Anderson, *All Our Losses, All Our Griefs,* pp. 136–137.

9. William Stafford, *Stories That Could Be True: New and Collected Poems* (New York: Harper & Row, 1977), p. 152.

10. William Stafford, *An Oregon Message* (New York: Harper & Row, 1987), p. 99.

11. Stafford, *Stories That Could Be True,* p. 32.

12. Ibid., pp. 62–63.

13. Ibid., p. 157.

14. Stafford, *An Oregon Message,* p. 38.

15. William Stafford, *A Glass Face in the Rain: New Poems* (New York: Harper & Row, 1982), p. 51.

16. Ibid., p. 45.

17. Stafford, *Stories That Could Be True,* p. 154.

18. Ibid., p. 204.

19. William Stafford, *Passwords* (New York: HarperCollins, 1991), p. 60.

20. Ibid., p. 69.

21. Stafford, *An Oregon Message,* p. 55.

22. Ibid., p. 57.

23. Stafford, *A Glass Face in the Rain*, p. 62.

24. Stafford, *Passwords*, p. 66.

25. Stafford, *A Glass Face in the Rain*, p. 103.

26. Stafford, *An Oregon Message*, p. 28.

27. Stafford, *Stories That Could Be True*, p. 90.

28. Ibid., p. 121.

29. Stafford, *Passwords*, p. 62.

30. Stafford, *A Glass Face in the Rain*, p. 93.

31. Stafford, *An Oregon Message*, p. 41.

32. Stafford, *Passwords*, p. 79.

33. Mitchell and Anderson, *All Our Losses, All Our Griefs*, p. 96.

34. Ibid.

35. William Stafford, *You Must Revise Your Life* (Ann Arbor, Mich.: The University of Michigan Press, 1986), p. 7.

36. Ibid., p. 8.

37. Stafford, *A Glass Face in the Rain*, p. 90.

38. Stafford, *Passwords*, p. 44.

39. Ibid., p. 36.

40. Ibid., p. 12.

41. Stafford, *Stories That Could Be True*, p. 93.

42. Stafford, *An Oregon Message*, p. 125.

43. Donald Capps, *Biblical Approaches to Pastoral Counseling* (Philadelphia: Westminster Press, 1981), pp. 93–95.

44. See Donald Capps, *Reframing: A New Method in Pastoral Care* (Minneapolis: Fortress Press, 1990), chs. 6–7.

CHAPTER 4

1. James Newton Poling, *The Abuse of Power: A Theological Problem* (Nashville: Abingdon Press, 1991), p. 187.

2. Ibid.

3. Ibid., pp. 72–73.

4. Ibid., p. 187.

5. Jeanne Stevenson Moessner and Maxine Glaz, "Introduction: I Heard a Cry," in Maxine Glaz and Jeanne Stevenson Moessner, eds., *Women in Travail and Transition: A New Pastoral Care* (Minneapolis: Fortress Press, 1991), pp. 1–2.

6. Ibid., p. 2.

7. Ibid.

8. Emma J. Justes, "Women," in Robert J. Wicks, Richard D. Parsons, and

Donald E. Capps, eds., *Clinical Handbook of Pastoral Counseling* (New York: Paulist Press, 1985), pp. 293–296.

9. Ibid., p. 296.

10. Denise Levertov, *Life in the Forest* (New York: New Directions Books, 1978), p. 115.

11. Denise Levertov, *Poems 1968–1972* (New York: New Directions Books, 1987), p. 215.

12. Denise Levertov, *New and Selected Essays* (New York: New Directions Books, 1992), p. 259.

13. Ibid., p. 260.

14. Ibid., pp. 260–261.

15. Ibid., p. 258.

16. Ibid., p. 247.

17. William Stafford, *Writing the Australian Crawl: Views on the Writer's Vocation* (Ann Arbor, Mich.: The University of Michigan Press, 1978), p. 146–147.

18. Ibid., p. 44.

19. Levertov, *Poems, 1968–1972*, p. 131.

20. Levertov, *Life in the Forest*, p. 27.

21. Ibid., p. 31.

22. Denise Levertov, *Candles in Babylon* (New York: New Directions Books, 1982), p. 44.

23. Levertov, *Life in the Forest*, pp. 41–42.

24. Denise Levertov, *A Door in the Hive* (New York: New Directions Books, 1989), p. 89.

25. Denise Levertov, *Oblique Prayers* (New York: New Directions Books, 1984), p. 35.

26. Denise Levertov, *Evening Train* (New York: New Directions Books, 1992), p. 59.

27. Levertov, *New and Selected Essays*, p. 261.

28. Denise Levertov, *Poems 1968–1972* (New York: New Directions Books, 1987), p. 112.

29. Ibid., p. 113.

30. Ibid., pp. 114–115.

31. Ibid., p. 118.

32. Denise Levertov, *Breathing the Water* (New York: New Directions Books, 1988), p. 25.

33. Levertov, *Evening Train*, p. 119.

34. Levertov, *New and Selected Essays*, p. 261.

35. Ibid.

36. Levertov, *Oblique Prayers*, p. 85.

37. Carl B. Rogers, *On Becoming a Person* (Boston: Houghton Mifflin, 1961), p. 26.

38. Levertov, *Poems 1960–1967*, p. 165.

39. Levertov, *Poems 1968–1972*, p. 62.

40. Levertov, *Breathing the Water*, p. 51.

41. Levertov, *Candles in Babylon*, pp. 82–83.

42. Levertov, *Evening Train*, p. 75.

43. Levertov, *Poems 1960–1967*, p. 163.

44. Levertov, *Breathing the Water*, p. 34.

45. Levertov, *Evening Train*, p. 19.

46. Levertov, *Candles in Babylon*, p. 7.

47. Levertov, *Life in the Forest*, p. 16.

48. Ibid., p. 95.

49. Levertov, *Poems 1968–1972*, p. 196.

50. Levertov, *A Door in the Hive*, p. 88.

51. Levertov, *Poems 1960–1967*, p. 196.

52. Levertov, *A Door in the Hive*, p. 4.

53. Levertov, *Evening Train*, p. 71.

54. Levertov, *Breathing the Water*, p. 38.

55. Levertov, *Evening Train*, p. 79.

56. Ibid., p. 80.

57. Levertov, *Poems 1960–1967*, p. 11.

58. Levertov, *Candles in Babylon*, p. 69.

59. Levertov, *Oblique Prayers*, p. 85.

60. Justes, "Women," in Wicks, Parsons, and Capps, eds., *Clinical Handbook of Pastoral Counseling*, p. 296.

61. David W. Augsburger, *Pastoral Counseling Across Cultures* (Philadelphia: Westminster Press, 1986), p. 13.

CHAPTER 5

1. Wayne E. Oates, *The Presence of God in Pastoral Counseling* (Waco, Tex.: Word Books, 1986), p. 32.

2. Ibid.

3. Ibid., pp. 32–33.

4. Ibid., p. 33.

5. Edward P. Wimberly, *Prayer in Pastoral Counseling: Suffering, Healing, and Discernment* (Louisville, Ky.: Westminster/John Knox Press, 1990), pp. 60–61.

6. Oates, *The Presence of God in Pastoral Counseling*, pp. 85–86.

7. Ibid., p. 86.

8. Ibid., p. 97. I also use the language of paradox in speaking of God in my *Reframing: A New Method in Pastoral Care* (Minneapolis: Fortress Press, 1990), pp. 166–168.

9. James Newton Poling, *The Abuse of Power: A Theological Problem* (Nashville: Abingdon Press, 1991), p. 166.

10. Ibid., p. 173.

11. Ibid.

12. Ibid., pp. 174–175.

13. Ibid., p. 175.

14. Ibid., p. 177.

15. Ibid., pp. 178–179.

16. Ibid., p. 176.

17. Levertov, *Breathing the Water*, p. 38.

18. Gerhard von Rad, *Wisdom in Israel*, trans. James D. Martin (London: SCM Press, 1972), p. 120.

19. Ibid., p. 129.

20. James L. Crenshaw, *Old Testament Wisdom: An Introduction* (Atlanta: John Knox Press, 1981), p. 125.

21. I have presented arguments for relating the biblical wisdom tradition to pastoral care in several books, including *Biblical Approaches to Pastoral Care* (Philadelphia: Westminster Press, 1981); *Life Cycle Theory and Pastoral Care* (Philadelphia: Fortress Press, 1983); and *Reframing*. See also Joan M. Erikson, *Wisdom and the Senses* (New York: W. W. Norton, 1988), ch. 7.

22. William Stafford, *An Oregon Message* (New York: Harper & Row, 1987), p. 115.

23. William Stafford, *Passwords* (New York: HarperCollins, 1991), p. 32.

24. Stafford, *An Oregon Message*, p. 110.

25. William Stafford, *Stories That Could Be True: New and Collected Poems* (New York: Harper & Row, 1977), p. 48.

26. Ibid., p. 41.

27. William Stafford, *A Glass Face in the Rain: New Poems* (New York: Harper & Row, 1982), p. 25.

28. Stafford, *Stories That Could Be True*, p. 31.

29. Ibid., p. 61.

30. Linda Metzger and Deborah A. Straub, eds., *Contemporary Authors*, New Revision Series, vol. 20 (Detroit: Gale Research, 1987), p. 441.

31. Ibid., pp. 441–442.

32. Walter J. Harrelson, "Wisdom and Pastoral Theology," *Andover Newton Quarterly* 7, no. 1 (1966): 6–14.

33. Stafford, *Stories That Could Be True*, p. 88.

34. Ibid., p. 166.

35. Ibid., p. 44.

36. Ibid., pp. 180–181.

37. Ibid., p. 196.

38. Ibid., pp. 248–249.

39. Metzger and Straub, eds., *Contemporary Authors*, p. 441.

40. Ibid.

41. Ibid.

42. Stafford, *Stories That Could Be True*, p. 46.

43. Ibid., p. 47.

44. Stafford, *A Glass Face in the Rain*, p. 43.

45. Stafford, *Stories That Could Be True*, pp. 197–198.

46. Ibid., p. 35.

47. Ibid., p. 73.

48. Stafford, *An Oregon Message*, p. 74.

49. Stafford, *Stories That Could Be True*, pp. 101–102.

50. Ibid., p. 56.

51. Stafford, *Passwords*, p. 81.

52. Stafford, *An Oregon Message*, p. 67.

53. Stafford, *Stories That Could Be True*, pp. 9–10.

54. Ibid., p. 239.

55. Ibid., p. 234.

56. Ibid., pp. 48–49.

57. Stafford, *Stories That Could Be True*, p. 193.

58. Ibid., p. 153.

59. Edward P. Wimberly and Anne Streaty Wimberly, *Liberation and Human Wholeness: The Conversion Experiences of Black People in Slavery and Freedom* (Nashville: Abingdon Press, 1986).

60. James E. Dittes, *The Male Predicament: On Being a Man Today* (San Francisco: Harper & Row, 1985), especially ch. 7, and his *When Work Goes Sour: A Male Perspective* (Philadelphia: Westminster Press, 1987), ch. 4.

61. Howard Clinebell, *Basic Types of Pastoral Care and Counseling* (Nashville: Abingdon Press, 1984), p. 72.

62. Stafford, *Stories That Could Be True*, p. 33.

63. See Linda Filippi, "Place, Feminism, and Healing: An Ecology of Pastoral Counseling," *The Journal of Pastoral Care* 45 (1991): 231–242. Her article concludes

with this eloquent affirmation of self and earth together: "In finding our authentic selves, in remembering how it feels to touch the earth, we will find that the heartbeat of the universe beats in us too, that our loving leads us to the holy, and that there is forgiveness. The heartbeat awaits. The choices are ours. The time is now. May we listen deeply and act with the wisdom of our whole selves."

64. Joseph Sittler, *The Care of the Earth and Other University Sermons* (Philadelphia: Fortress Press, 1964), p. 89.

65. Stafford, *Stories That Could Be True*, p. 53.

66. Stafford, *A Glass Face in the Rain*, p. 33.

67. In a recent study of clergy and laity views of sins and virtues, I found that 20 percent of the laity judged wisdom ("The conducting of one's life in a wise and thoughtful manner; to live responsibly and to exercise good judgment in the concerns of everyday life") to be the most desirable virtue, while only 6 percent of the clergy judged it so. See Donald Capps, "The Deadly Sins and Saving Virtues: How They Are Viewed by Laity," *Pastoral Psychology* 37 (1989): 229–253; idem, "The Deadly Sins and Saving Virtues: How They Are Viewed by Clergy," *Pastoral Psychology* 40 (1992): 209–233.

68. See, for example, William Hudson O'Hanlon and Michele Weiner-Davis, *In Search of Solutions: A New Direction in Psychotherapy* (New York: W. W. Norton, 1989), pp. 29–30. Also, Paul Watzlawick, John Weakland, and Richard Fisch, *Change: Principles of Problem Formation and Problem Resolution* (New York: W. W. Norton, 1974), ch. 3.

INDEX

Poems by William Stafford are marked (WS). Poems by Denise Levertov are marked (DL).